A Brown Paper School Book

WORD WORKS

Why the Alphabet Is a Kid's Best Friend

Cathryn Berger Kaye

Illustrated by
Martha Weston

Little, Brown and Company
Boston   Toronto

This Brown Paper School book was edited and
prepared for publication at The Yolla Bolly Press,
Covelo, California, during the spring and summer of 1984. The
series is under the supervision of James and Carolyn
Robertson. Editorial and production staff: Patricia
Houden Gunther, Dan Hibshman, Juliana
Yoder, and Barbara Youngblood.

Library of Congress Cataloging in Publication Data

Kaye, Cathy Berger.
Word works.

(A Brown paper school book)
Summary: Explores the way words are used in everyday
life, in talking, writing, communicating, and thinking,
as well as in creating stories and poems, printing books,
playing games, and programming computers.
1. Language arts (Elementary)—Juvenile literature.
2. Vocabulary—Juvenile literature. [1. Language arts.
2. Communication. 3. Creative writing. 4. Word games.]
I. Weston, Martha, ill. II. Title.
LB1576.K375 1985   372.6   84-17154
ISBN 0-316-48376-1
ISBN 0-316-48375-3 (pbk.)

HC: 10 9 8 7 6 5 4 3
PB: 10 9 8 7 6 5 4 3

First edition. Published simultaneously in Canada
by Little, Brown & Company (Canada) Limited.
Printed in the United States of America.

Contents

A Short and Wordy Introduction

This book is about words—why we have them, why we need them, how we use them. Your mouth is full of words and so are your ears. If you haven't thought much about the ways words work, now's your chance.

Words are tools. You can build castles in the air with some highfalutin words or craft a tiny poem for your friend's valentine. You can invent new words and find lost ones or make a record of current events to bury inside a time capsule.

Words are like friends. When you are alone you can play games with them or use them to write a letter to a pal. When you're with friends you can write and stage a play or start your own newspaper.

There are words that sound like music: hallelujah, bebop, and mariachi. Some words are fun just to say, like popcorn, abracadabra, and stegosaurus. Words can make you laugh when you hear a ridiculous riddle or a silly story. They can even bring tears to your eyes in a sad song or a romantic rhyme.

If you go on a trip, words come along for the ride without taking up any space. They get along fine without sleep and don't eat much. If you get lost, they help you get found. Thousands of words are just waiting for you to put them to work . . . or play.

Chapter One
Words to the Wise

You make choices all the time—which clothes to put on in the morning, which friend to be with, which movie to see, which kind of spin to put on a baseball. Endless choices. You may not think about it, but you are always choosing words too; and there are many to choose. About 1,000,000 words make up the English language. Each time you talk, write, or think, you choose among all the words you know. If you're like the average person, you have a stockpile of about 3,000 words that you use on a regular basis.

The Right Word

Some of your word choices seem to be automatic; you don't stop to think about them, but somehow the right words just come out. Sometimes a word escapes you or sits right on the tip of your tongue.

Much of your life has been spent learning about words—what they mean, what they look like, and how they go together. You hear sounds even before you're born. After you are born, sounds surround you—the hmmmmm of the refrigerator, the ring of the telephone, the whir of passing traffic, the honking of horns, the falling rain, and, of course, the sounds of humans. As a baby, you begin to exercise your lips and imitate sounds until you can shape words. Ask your family what your first words were; even though you were there, you may not remember.

Even after you begin to say some words, you still have to figure out what other words mean: that thing you put on your foot is a shoe, the one for your head is a cap, and on and on. You find out how to say yes and no and stop and go and help.

You start with single words. Soon you are combining words two at a time, then three, and before you know it you have a phrase: Me want go store.

In no time at all, you have mastered a language. You know what the sounds are, how they are put together, and what they mean. You can say: I want to go to the store. You can combine words to make an endless number of sentences.

See supper fly!

Tricky Words

Using language may sound pretty easy, especially since you've done it and so have millions of other people. However, the English language has its share of tricks and troubles that make it pretty difficult at times.

For example, some words sound the same but look different. Can you bake a cake using "flower"? If you were riding a horse, could you pull on the "rains" to make it stop?

Words can look the same and sound different. If you tear your pants, you could end up with a tear in your eye. If you got the lead in a school play, you might get nervous and break the lead in your pencil.

To make matters even more complicated, words may look the same, sound the same, but have different meanings, depending on how you use them. Two

friends might share a glass of punch, then start punching each other. When taking a trip, don't trip on your luggage! You can run a flag up a flagpole, get a run in your stocking, and score a run in a baseball game.

Sometimes the way words are combined just doesn't make sense. Take the word *houseboat*—a boat that is a house. Now, what about housecat? Is that a cat that is a house? If you sleep over, it doesn't mean you will oversleep. And if a magnifying glass magnifies, does a looking glass look?

Words don't always mean what they seem to mean. To coin a phrase has absolutely nothing to do with money. Singing a few bars has nothing at all to do with soap.

This may sound peculiar, but words actually don't mean a thing. Nothing at all—that is, until intelligent people, such as you and I, give them meaning.

How many hares are on your head?

Meet the Kamot

To meet the Kamot, get a piece of paper and colored drawing pens. Divide your paper into six squares, numbering them from 1 to 6.

The Kamot is described in six parts. First, read only number 1. Then, based on the information given in number 1, draw a picture in the first square of what you think a Kamot looks like. When you finish, read number 2 and draw a picture in the second square. Continue reading each description then drawing a picture until you have read and drawn number 6. Here goes.

I hope it isn't scary!

1	2	3
4	5	6

1. The Kamot is a rare and special animal with four legs and two short ears. (Draw a Kamot in square 1.)

2. Being light green, a Kamot blends into the grass while hunting for its food. Its tail is actually an antenna that keeps it from bumping into objects at night. (Draw your second Kamot.)

3. A member of the cat family, the Kamot outsizes the lion two and a half times. Kamots usually travel in groups of three to five. (Draw a third Kamot.)

4. A baby Kamot can walk within hours of its birth. At first it hardly looks like a Kamot because it doesn't yet have long hair. (Now draw a fourth Kamot.)

5. A Kamot with whiskers? Never. And only females have tufts of fur on top of their heads; all males are bald. (Draw a fifth Kamot; only one more to go.)

6. Kamots are easily identified by their giant paws, each of which has seven toes. Kamots make wonderful pets. They are strict vegetarians, and they enjoy warmth and attention from humans. (Draw your sixth and final Kamot.)

Look back at your six drawings. Is each of them different? The five letters that spell Kamot don't tell you about its size or color or that it makes a great pet. But once you find out that information, the word creates an image for you—a mental picture—and has meaning.

Now here's some bad news. You cannot buy a Kamot at your local pet store, and you can't find one at the zoo. It's an imaginary beast. The good news is that you can introduce the Kamot to other people and see if their Kamots look like yours.

The Good Egg — Mr. H.D.

Humpty Dumpty sat on a wall; Humpty Dumpty had a great fall—is that all? Nope. In *Through the Looking-Glass* by Lewis Carroll, Humpty Dumpty is quite the scholarly fellow, tossing words around with Alice. In fact, when she's not quite sure whether he's using them properly, he explains to her:

"When *I* use a word," Humpty Dumpty said, in a rather scornful tone, "it means just what I choose it to mean—neither more nor less."

"The question is," said Alice, "whether you *can* make words mean so many different things."

"The question is," said Humpty Dumpty, "which is to be master—that's all. . . . When I make a word do a lot of work, I always pay it extra."

Using Mr. H.D.'s approach to words, you could assign new meanings to words whenever you wanted to. You could tell someone: "This dinner tastes miraculous!" When you say "miraculous," you mean "it could bounce higher than a tennis ball." That's a long meaning, even for a ten-letter word. According to H.D.'s payment method, that word might cost you as much as $1.50.

How confused would you be if the meanings of words kept changing? How could you ever be sure what your friends were talking about?

Well, even if the good egg's method isn't practical, he has a point: Words can take on different meanings with each person who uses them. We must control the words we use, or they may end up controlling us.

Words That Cost a Lot

Humpty Dumpty used a pay-as-you-use-words method. Do you have any idea how much that would cost you?

Can you imagine getting a bill from a word?

Dear Friend,

You have used me 2,475 times in the last ten years. I charge 25 cents a shot, so you owe me $618.75. Pay immediately. Thanks.

Strange

Who's that from?

I can't say. It's too expensive.

That's strange.

Shh!!!

Words could make quite a bit of money at that rate. If words did charge for their use, which ones do you think would be the wealthiest? Following are the ten most frequently used words in the English language:

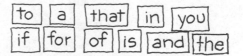

to a that in you
if for of is and the

For fun, rank them according to their popularity. Number 1 would be the word used most often, number 2, the second-most-often-used word, and so on. (You can find the answers in the back of the book.)

Examine something you have written, perhaps a homework assignment from your English or history class. How many times do those words appear in it? Can you write a paragraph without using them at all?

Remember that there are a million words out there to choose from. Why should you use the same ones over and over again? One thing is certain, if you don't know a word, you won't use it.

The Word Bank

Right now you have a word stockpile that may have only 2,864 words in it. How many new words would you gather if you learned one word every day for a year? three years? five years? sixty-five years?

You decide to be a "word banker" and add words to your collection. It's easy to open an account. First, get a notebook. Then write these headings on the first page.

Date	New Word	Meaning

Then search out new words. You'll find them everywhere—in books, on TV, slipping into conversations, and at school—they're all over.

Make an entry every day. If you aren't certain about the meaning, ask someone or look it up in a dictionary. (See "A Meaning: Look It Up" in Chapter 9.)

Be sure to use your word-bank words. Drop one at the dinner table as you eat your esculent mashed potatoes, or discuss with your friends what it's like to be an abecedarian as you walk to school. People will begin to wonder what you are up to. Just like your savings account, you will begin to collect interest daily.

12

How Many Languages?

While you are busy making sense out of the English language, people all over the world are learning and speaking other languages. Can you guess how many languages are spoken in the world? Remember, you live on a planet that has seven continents that are divided into more than 160 countries, with approximately 4,700,000,000 people. Begin your count by thinking of all the languages you've ever heard about. Next, get a world map or a globe. Find a country and check your list. For example, do you think the people in Afghanistan speak one of the languages already on your list? How about the people of Brazil, Madagascar, and Finland? Encyclopedias, dictionaries, and almanacs can help you answer your language-count questions.

Back to how many languages. If you guessed that there are between 3,000 and 5,000 languages used around the world today, you're right on target. If those languages were divided equally among the world's population, how many people would speak each language? But languages aren't divided like that. Some are spoken by millions of people, others by several thousand. Then there are languages such as Eyak. How many people speak Eyak? Three, at last count. All of them are native Alaskans. If you want to find someone who speaks Manx, you're out of luck. The last Manx speaker died in the British Isles in 1974.

Which language do you think is used by the most people? Can you pick the top three? (The answers are in the back of the book.) How many of these languages do you know?

13

Why are there so many languages? Ever since people began walking around on this planet, they have developed languages as a means to get messages from one person to another. Each separate group figured out its own way to speak, and, in some cases, to write. The majority of languages in the world are spoken only; they have no written form.

Languages differ one from another. With 3,000 languages, it's nearly impossible to learn them all, though some people can master as many as 60. You can be certain there will always be languages you won't know, but don't let that stop you from learning 1, 2, 3, or more.

With every language you learn, you add to the number of people throughout the world you can talk to. You can read more books, watch more plays, and make more friends. You can discuss sports, foods, or share some of your favorite expressions.

You already have a head start on speaking other languages. Surprised? Read on:

What a day! I jump out of bed, quickly change from pajamas to dungarees, grab a banana, and I'm out the door. Off to the carnival. Suddenly, I catch sight of strolling guitars and a llama riding in a coach. A man wearing camouflage khakis calls the crowd to see a safari film. A woman riding a giraffe recites limericks. Food booths sell steamed artichokes, barbecued sandwiches, potato salad, noodle pudding, hot chowder, iced tea, and pecan ice cream. Then I remember my algebra test and head home. On the way out I buy a sack of taffy to help me study.

14

There once was a kid from Brisbane, who knew languages fancy and plain. But...

The story you have just read contains words from many languages, words that have been adopted by the English language. Check the list.

algebra — Arabic
artichoke — Arabic
banana — West African
barbecue — Arawak
camouflage — French
carnival — Italian
chowder — French
coach — Hungarian
giraffe — Arabic
guitar — Spanish
khakis — Urdu
limericks — Irish
llama — Spanish
noodle — German
pajamas — Hindi
pecan — Algonquian
potato — Dutch
sack — Hebrew
safari — Swahili
taffy — West Indian
tea — Chinese

The list goes on and on. Of course, knowing a language is different from being familiar with a few words, but it's a start.

A Universal Language

Are all these languages really necessary? They do create confusion. Would you prefer one language common to all people worldwide?

Lazarus Ludwig Zamenhof thought that a universal language would help people get along better by eliminating the confusion and misunderstandings that can occur with translations. He decided to do something. Using bits and pieces of all the languages he knew—Polish, German, Russian, English, Latin, Greek, Hebrew, French, and Yiddish—Zamenhof created a new language. In 1887 he put the finishing touches on a new language with a twenty-eight-letter alphabet. Using the name Dr. Esperanto, he mailed brochures announcing his accomplishment. The word *esperanto,* meaning "one who hopes," stuck to the language. Now several million people speak Esperanto, and it's taught in approximately 600 schools around the world.

Would you be willing to give up English for a universal language? If you did, what would disappear with it? It's something to think about.

Chapter Two
The Written Word

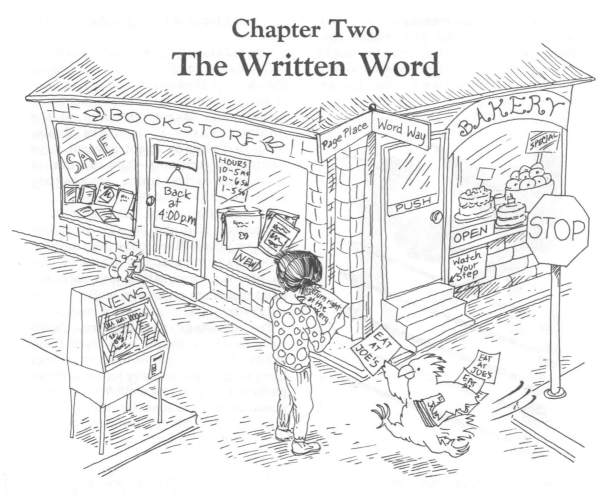

Writing pops up in your life all the time: a phone message, a letter, an invitation, a thank-you note, a cereal-box coupon, a fill-in-the-blanks story. You see writing almost everywhere you go.

Have you ever wondered why people write? Writing is one way we can remember thoughts and experiences and keep track of which crops were planted where in the garden. Some people jot down a feeling or write a description of a special event. Some people write messages for future generations. Time capsules are filled with writing: plays, dictionaries, history books, and movie scripts. They can be marked "Open me in the year 2479." (That's really planning for the future.) Other people are satisfied with just being able to write messages for people today, but they want their messages to be big enough to be seen for miles and miles. Skywriting works for them.

Mixed Messages

Even before the days of writing, people wanted to send messages to each other. Here's a story of one such attempt.

About 2,500 years ago, a Persian general named Darius invaded the land of the Scythians, early inhabitants of what is now southern Russia. The Scythians sent Darius a "letter" consisting of whole objects: a bird, a mouse, a frog, and five arrows. Darius assumed this meant "victory" because

Try to make a rebus. Turn a poem, song, riddle, or rhyme into a combination of pictures and words. Leave spaces between the words, and use a + sign to link sounds that form a single word. Here is a rebus rhyme to get you started. (The rhyme is "translated" at the back of the book.)

I sure agree with that!

I don't know... It might be fun.

I never ⟨saw⟩ a ⟨cat⟩ Purrr + pull ⟨cow⟩

I never hope 2 C 1

But I ⟨can⟩ tell U N + ⟨leg⟩ + how

I + d ⟨rat⟩ + her C T + ⟨hand⟩ B 1 !

The Evolution of the A

Imagine you are the letter *A*. Where did you come from? How did you end up first in the line of twenty-six letters that make up the English alphabet?

You're rather old, you know. You began as an ox—that's right. Not every letter can claim such dignified beginnings. First, you were a picture of an ox, and you meant just that: an ox. Let's say, perhaps, that a farmer had four oxen and wanted to sell all of them. The farmer could carry a sign with four of your pictures on it through the marketplace.

Your picture was used so often and became so popular that finally people decided from then on the drawing of an ox would represent the sound *ah*. No more ox. From then on the drawing was a letter.

Something like this really took place thousands of years ago in a land called Phoenicia, which was located on the eastern shores of the Mediterranean Sea. The Phoenicians had many letters, and you, old ox, were one of them.

The Phoenicians sailed the Mediterranean Sea and traded with many people, including the Greeks. On one of their trips, the sailors took you along, and the Greeks were so impressed with you and the other letters that they kept you with them.

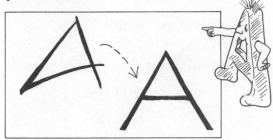

Naturally, the Greeks made a few changes. They didn't think you looked quite right as you were, so they flipped you over, and, presto, you looked like our English *A*. The Greeks gave you a new name, *alpha,* and also overhauled your best friend, *beta.* They put you two together in front of the other letters: alpha + beta = alphabet.

There you were—number 1—and you have stayed that way ever since. You and your gang of letters also became popular in Rome. The Romans altered your shapes a bit and gave you something to stand on—little feet, or serifs. These Roman serifs can still be found on many pages, including the ones in this book.

Write Like a Scribe

Thousands of years ago there were no printing presses. Writing was the job of people called *scribes.* Greek scribes were able to make large letters look balanced and in good proportion. To make a writing implement similar to the one used by early Greeks, take two pencils and a small, rectangular-shaped object made of a sturdy substance such as wood or plastic. The rectangular-shaped object acts as a brace between the two pencils. Use tape, string, or a rubber band to join them together. By holding the pencils at different angles, you can become highly skilled at making inscriptions of all shapes and sizes—like a real scribe.

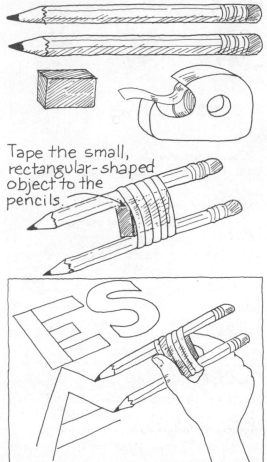

Tape the small, rectangular-shaped object to the pencils.

To England, To England

Eventually, the letters of the Roman alphabet were carried by way of war and religion to England. People there used the newfangled letters to write and record the Old English language, a grandparent of the language we speak and write today. Here are some examples of Old English spelling:

cild
gear
niht
brycg
fyr
heofon
ceald
cwen
cyta
merscmealwe

Can you read them? Here is how we would write the same words today:

child
year
night
bridge
fire
heaven
cold
queen
kite
marshmallow

As the written and spoken language continued to change, Old English became Middle English. How do you think these Middle English words would be written today?

streem
depe
nozle
dimpul

Today we would write:

stream
deep
nozzle
dimple

By the year 1450—more than 500 years ago—the modern English language that we know had developed, but it has continued to change. Modern English traveled across oceans, farther and farther from its origins. Western English, the language used in the United States, has distinct differences from its English cousin. Here are a few spelling differences.

British English	Western English
storey	story
cheque	check
grey	gray
waggon	wagon
colour	color
theatre	theater

Meanings also differ, depending on which side of the Atlantic you're on.

British English	Western English
cue up	stand in line
ride a lift	ride an elevator
bonnet	hood of a car

The Armadillo Race

What do you think? Was it worth the time and effort of thousands of people over thousands of years to create the writing system we use? If there is any question in your mind, take a piece of paper, a pencil, and a timepiece. A friend would also be helpful. Give your friend the timepiece; you keep the paper and pencil. Have your friend time you while you do each of the following:

1. Draw a picture of an armadillo.
2. Write the word *armadillo*.

Okay, which was faster, more efficient, and without a question *armadillo?*

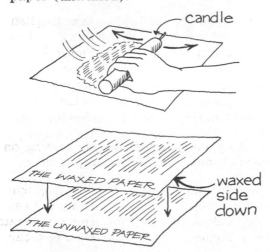

Wax-Paper Sandwiches

Greeks and Romans used waxed sheets for sending messages. Try it yourself by using a piece of paper and a candle. Rub the candle on the paper to form a coating. Place the waxed sheet wax side down on a second piece of paper (unwaxed).

candle

THE WAXED PAPER

waxed side down

THE UNWAXED PAPER

Try a ballpoint pen.

Write your message on your "wax-paper sandwich." Make sure you press hard. You may want to experiment with different writing tools to get a clear imprint.

Give the paper with the invisible wax lines to your friend. Instruct him or her to place finely ground coffee or charcoal powder on the paper, then shake off the excess. The message remains.

some kind of dark powdery stuff

THE ARMADILLO WILL NOT BE SEEN UNTIL THE SUN HAS GONE FROM THE OUTER ROCKS.
OLGA

hmm...

The message revealed. (*This* one must be in a code!)

Invisible Writing

This trick takes something that is invisible, then makes it visible. Using common household foods, you can create your own appearing act with words. The supplies you need are: paper, an empty fountain pen or a toothpick, and lemon juice.

Dip the pen in the lemon juice and write. After the paper dries, hold it close to a light bulb. The warmth of the bulb heats the "ink," causing it to appear dramatically before your eyes. You may have to wait five minutes for the writing to become visible.

If this message is between you and a friend, try the read-between-the-lines technique. Use regular ink to write a nonsecret note, then write invisibly between the visible lines.

Codes and Ciphers

It's no secret that people sometimes want to write secret messages to each other. Secret messages using codes and ciphers have been used for thousands of years.

Codes substitute whole words or symbols for the real words or phrases. Let's say, for example, that you and I have a secret agreement: Whenever I write "at the store," I really mean "in the park"; and if I mention a time, such as 3:00, I always mean two hours later. Now, on your way out of school, you find this note on your bicycle seat: "Meet me at the store at 1:30 this afternoon. See you then, James." The real message is between you and me; it's our code.

A cipher is different. Again, it's a planned agreement, but with a few more surprises. A simple cipher can involve switching letters of the alphabet—writing *b* for *a, c* for *b, d* for *c,* and so on, always using the next letter in the alphabet instead of the correct one. Instead of using the letters on top, write the ones underneath.

a b c d e f g h i j k l m n o p q r s t u v w x y z
b c d e f g h i j k l m n o p q r s t u v w x y z a

My message to you is: J xbjufe bu uif gpvoubjo, cvu zpv xfsf mbuf.

To be able to conjure up a combination of codes and ciphers that will be difficult to ''break'' involves practice and imagination. Breaking a code or cipher doesn't happen when you drop it; it happens when someone figures out how the code or cipher works. (If you can't decipher the message above, look in the back of the book.)

A Cipher Wheel

A cipher wheel has letters on a metal cylinder, which is turned to hide or confide messages. Who has used them? The Spartans of ancient Greece and Thomas Jefferson, the third president of the United States. You, too, can use a cipher wheel if you follow the instructions below.

You will need an empty toilet paper tube, a pen, tape, a pair of scissors, and a piece of paper. Cut a ½-inch strip of paper, about 10 inches long. Tape down one end. Wrap the paper snugly around the tube so the edges of the paper touch each other. Using the pen, write your secret message so that one letter falls on a separate paper column. You can write several lines of messages if you like.

Remove the paper strip and lay it out flat. Pass the strip and the tube to your friend. When he or she wraps the paper snugly around the tube and turns the wheel, your message will be revealed.

When you get the hang of it, experiment with different sizes of message holders. Round shapes work best. Try a long piece of wooden dowel for extra-long messages.

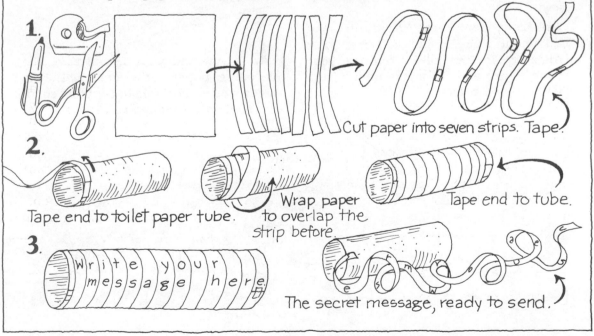

1. Cut paper into seven strips. Tape.

2. Tape end to toilet paper tube. Wrap paper to overlap the strip before. Tape end to tube.

3. Write your message here. The secret message, ready to send.

Create-a-Code

Here are several more ideas to get you going with cryptography—secret writing. Once you understand the basics, you can have fun inventing your own codes and ciphers.

🧀 SWISS CHEESE IT 🧀

1. Get a few pieces of paper, several pens, a pair of scissors, and a friend. Draw a Swiss-cheese design on a piece of paper, making the "holes" big enough to hold a word. Using your pattern, cut the holes out of two sheets of paper, one for you and one for your friend.

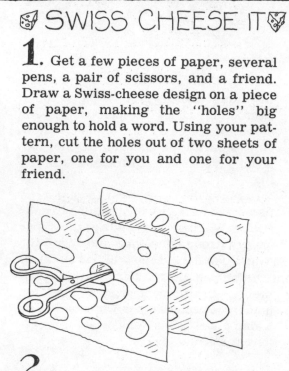

2. Lay your "cheese" paper on top of an uncut piece of paper. Write your message in the holes. Remove your code paper and fill in the uncut page with other words.

3. Hand the written sheet to your friend. When she or he places a cheese paper on top of it, your message should be clear.

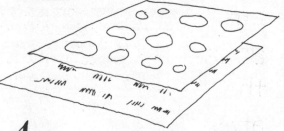

4. If you and your friend save the decoding papers, the ones with the holes, you will be able to continue sending each other hidden messages.

PICTO-CODE

You and your friends can develop your own secret written symbols. Replace words with symbols so no one else will be able to figure out your messages. Use these symbols, or make up your own.

I	⊙
house	⋏
cry	!/!\
before	↶
we	⋓
over	⋅⋅
am	⋀
going	→
the	—
after	⤳
me	◱
come	⋈
a	⋃
far	⌇⤳
and	⊥
you	◁
want	△

...Okay, if I draw a square with a dot inside it means "today" if the dot is outside the on the left it m erday, but o the right side then it m

Read this message:

> ⊙⋏ → to my ⋏. ↶ ⊙ leave, ⊙△ to know, can ◱ ⋈ ⋅⋅ ?

As you write your messages, be sure to leave spaces between the symbols for easier decoding.

Instead of signing your name to a message, you might want to make up your own secret symbol to use.

NICE ARE NICE

Graffiti – Imported from Italy?

Graffiti are made by locals, but the word is imported. This type of writing on the wall comes from an Italian word meaning "scribbling" or "scratching," and has even been found on the ancient ruins of Pompeii.

TIC-TAC-TOE CODE

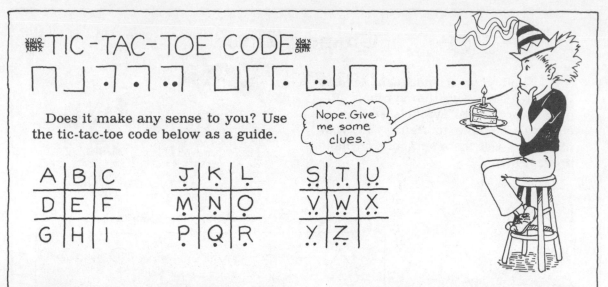

Does it make any sense to you? Use the tic-tac-toe code below as a guide.

Nope. Give me some clues.

A	B	C
D	E	F
G	H	I

J.	K.	L.
M.	N.	O.
P.	Q.	R.

:S	:T	:U
:V	:W	:X
:Y	:Z	

Each letter of the alphabet is on one of the three tic-tac-toe grids. To spell a word in code, look at where the letter sits, then draw the lines that appear around it. Some letters also have dots in their spaces. Look at these three letters.

A = ⌐   N = □·   Y = ·.·

Get it? Now try decoding the two words written in tic-tac-toe code. (Look in the back of the book for the answer if you can't figure out the message.)

Could you expand this code to include numbers?

WORD HISTORY

Take a Quiz on a Bet?

James Daly did. This theater manager from Dublin, Ireland, bet he could invent a new word and make it the talk of the town in just one day. He hired young people to paint the word *quiz* on every wall they could find while the rest of the town slept. Guess what everyone was talking about the next morning? The new word came to mean ''a test of knowledge,'' and a short one at that.

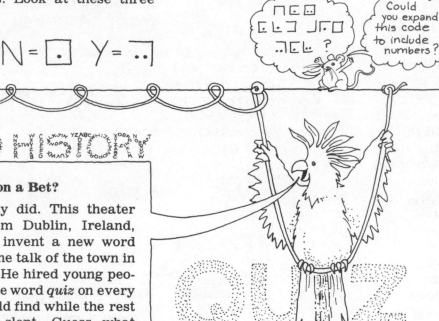

Chapter Three
Language Works

Archers use bows and arrows to make their mark. Slowly they draw back on the bow, with full concentration and steady aim on the bull's-eye. When aim is certain, the arrow is released to make its way to the target.

Language is your bow and arrow for reaching the target of communication —delivery of a message. Language is a system of do's and don'ts, guidelines, and rules. These structure language in an organized manner, keeping you on target, so you get a bull's-eye often.

What's a Grammar?

You live with rules all around you. There's a rule about what time you have to be at school in the morning and one about how old you must be to legally drive a car. You may have a rule in your family about how many hours of television you can watch per day or how many slices of pizza you can eat before bedtime. You may make a rule by adding a new boundary line in a game of soccer or tag. Rules help give form and shape to what you do. They serve as guides and agreements among the people who use them.

But *Dad*, you *never* said there was a *rule* about fishbowls and heads!

It follows that languages, too, have rules. All languages do, and English has its full share. Don't fret. You know most of the rules already; in fact, by the age of eight you have learned the rules simply by using English. You've been a kind of sponge, absorbing rules while you learned how to talk and write.

If you wanted to sell a box of English language rules, you could get a container, place all the rules inside, then figure out how to label your product. You could make up your own word or use the one that's been around for some time now: *grammar*. Rules of grammar hold a language together, creating a common ground for sending messages. There are more grammar rules than the ones mentioned here, but take a glance and see if you already know these.

Probably the most important rule is that English is a word-order language. This rule evolved long ago while people were making certain agreements based on their personal opinion of what they liked and disliked.

Even if that particular conversation didn't happen, the changes did occur. They happened over many years and probably involved many folks. The bottom line is that English acquired order, and you learned it. See if you can figure out these unordered English sentences. Sequence the words to fit your language rules. Use all the words given for each sentence. (The answers are in the back of the book.)

1. ride this day is great bike a for a.

2. show tonight park at fireworks there's the a.

3. buying for stamps me the thanks for.

4. walked needs the be to dog away right.

English-speaking people get accustomed to a certain sound and sequencing. Phrasing different from what we are used to sounds strange, but the strange can become acceptable if many people start using it and agree that it is correct. That's one way language changes.

Language also has rules that keep wordsseparatefromeachotherwhenyou writethem. When you speak, you pause between words, sometimes ever so briefly. When writing, you leave visible space between words to make it easier for the reader. That's another rule.

There are many more rules where these came from.

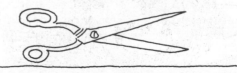

A Comma, a Pair of Scissors, and a Movie Director

All three have to do with cutting. *Comma* comes from the Greek word *komma,* meaning "a piece cut off." That's what it does in a sentence. The *cis* in s*cis*sors is Latin, meaning "to cut." And movie directors call out "Cut!" when they want to stop the action.

To the Point

When you speak, the sound, or inflection, of your voice adds a great deal to the meaning of the words you say.

Quickly spoken words express your excitement.

Very hushed tones say you have a secret.

When you ask a question your voice often rises at the end of the phrase, right?

A statement of fact may have a flatter sound.

With the written word, you lose the advantage of varying sounds of speech. You're limited to what's on paper to convey your truest meaning. However, to your aid come handy shapes especially designed for the purpose of being sound monitors on paper. These marvelous creations are called *punctuation,* which means "putting in points." You've seen them plenty of times; in fact, there are five different ones in this paragraph alone.

Let's examine several kinds of punctuation and determine each one's special use.

. That's all it is, a single dot, but a very powerful one. Each time you put one on paper, you're directing your reader to come to a complete stop. Actually, a ., or period, is very much like a stop sign, which signals cars to make a full stop. If the period weren't there, sentences would collide with each other there would be no telling where one ends and another begins that would mean mass confusion among all the written words to protect these innocent unprotected words keep in mind when you use a period you create the sound of STOP.

, The comma, a dot with a tail, is probably the most frequently used sentence signal of all. Its message is quite clear: Slow down, pause a moment. It's a reminder too: Hey, I'm not done, there's more to come.

! When you have an exclamation to make, pull out the most exuberant mark you can: Let it shout! That's what this dot below a line, an exclamation mark, does—it cries out and lets the full voice of the written word be heard. Can you hear the difference between these two sentences:

There's a fire in the basement.

There's a fire in the basement!

One will certainly attract more attention than the other. This mark is used to show excitement, fun, and danger. Use it sparingly to get the full impact; otherwise everything may sound like a fire in the basement.

? What's that? It's an unmistakable sound—the questioning voice. The trusty curl with a dot, or question mark, has a special job, one of asking. It means that something is up in the air. It asks you to wake up, listen, and figure it out. Usually the ? indicates a rise in the sound of the voice, a lift at the end of the sentence. Does that make sense?

Punctuation is correct when it accurately conveys the intention of your writing. So take control with the . , ! ? and see what happens.

The First Boycott

In 1880 Captain Charles Cunningham Boycott raised the rents in County Mayo, Ireland, and got quite a surprise: The local folks fought back—and not with violence. They refused to sell him goods in stores or to deliver his mail. Although he wasn't in personal danger, he left for England when his property was damaged. The story made news: A Boycott! Today the word describes a nonviolent strategy for making social change. It's a plan for not doing something: not buying from a store if the owner isn't fair to employees or not attending classes at a university if the tuition goes up too high. That's a *boycott*.

It's Going in the Wrong Direction

In the early 1900s when automobiles were invented, there were just a few cars on the road, but then more and more people began to drive these noisy contraptions. It was enough to scare a good horse off the road.

There were problems to solve. What could be done to prevent drivers from steering their cars into each other? One solution was to divide the roads with painted lines and to instruct drivers to stay to the right of the lines. Or is it to the left? Different countries have settled on different rules. That means it's up to you, the driver, to know the rules and drive safely.

What does all this have to do with words? Readers and writers need to know the rules of the written road, or they may end up going in the wrong direction. Are there traffic tickets for writing backwards?

Early Greek writing went in two directions—first to the right, then to the left—like an ox pulling a plow in a field. It had plenty of turns, like this:

First it went in one
ti neht dna noitcerid
went the other way.
si gnitirw fo dnik sihT
called *boustrophedon,*
.nexo ekil gninrut ro

Maybe all this back and forth made people dizzy, since this way of writing didn't last. The turns were thrown out, and left-to-right became the rule of the road—the written road, that is.

A language could be written in almost any direction: left to right, right to left, top to bottom, bottom to top. Do you know of languages that go in each of these directions?

Do you think it's hard to keep track of what you are reading when you have to keep turning the book to find out what the words say?

34

See how quickly your friends catch on. Pick a new direction for writing and print a message. Try the one-of-a-kind Rongo-rongo writing used by the people on Easter Island.

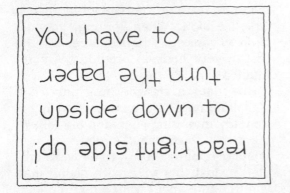

You have to
turn the paper
upside down to
read right side up!

Can your friends read it?

Which Way? ?Yaw hcihW

Leonardo da Vinci (1452-1519) had plenty of big ideas. This Italian painter, engineer, sculptor, and architect designed aircraft long before the Wright brothers' first flight and tried to figure out the inner workings of the human body. He wanted his work to be private, so he created his own secret language by writing backwards.

He wrote backwards.

You can become a backward pro with just a bit of practice. Begin by writing the entire alphabet forward, then backwards. Next try a word, a phrase, a sentence, then an entire message.

Writing backwards can be
confusing.
Reading it can be amusing.
I use it cause without a doubt
I can't write inside out!

Hints for reading backward writing:
1. Hold the message up to a mirror and read the reflection.
2. Hold your paper so the side with the words is facing a light bulb or the sun. If your paper is not too thick, you should be able to read right through the paper.

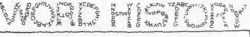

Turning Green Around the Edges?

You had better check because if you're growing, that's what is happening. To *grow* really means to "become green."

A Language of Signs

Could a language system be completely silent and still effectively send messages? Remove writing as an option. Does that change your opinion?

Before sounds were used to send messages, people used gestures—with hands and body movements. You use them today by waving hello to friends, frowning displeasure, and using the umpire's "you're out" signal. Watch a toddler for awhile and you'll see a person who communicates well with gestures and body movements. Some people call these gestures body language.

For people who are deaf or unable to produce vocal sound, hand and body gestures are a visual language, a way to send and receive messages. Each specific physical gesture that conveys meaning from one person to another is called a *sign*. When signing, you depend on your eyes, hands, face, and the rest of your body to provide the communication.

How does a sign become part of a sign language? To answer that question, try inventing signs for the following words: car, drink, smile, you, me, telephone, baby. Many signs were created in just this way, with people like you thinking about what would be logical and easy to remember. Other words are not so obvious, words such as cow, girl, boy, mother, slow. Still they get invented, sometimes because of an association that gets lost over time. New signs become popular because of frequent use and general acceptance, just as new *words* come into our language. Signing and speech change with the times.

Sign language, as well as verbal language, has inflections; they are visual and are indicated by gestures and expressions. At the end of signing a question, you can raise your eyebrows or keep your hands up. To underline or emphasize a word or phrase, you can make the gesturing movements stronger and/or larger.

When there isn't a sign available for what you want to say, fingerspelling comes in handy. Fingerspelling is a code where the hand forms a shape that represents a letter. Each letter in the word is shaped individually. It is useful especially with names and technical words. Of course, using a sign for a word is faster and more efficient than fingerspelling. Having both at your disposal means you can communicate absolutely everything.

If you like using your hands, learning to sign can be fun and challenging. It's hard work, but you will join millions of people all over the world who use visual communication. Whether or not your ears are capable of hearing sound is not what truly matters; it's what is between your ears that is important.

A HANDFUL OF LETTERS

The fingerspelling alphabet can best be taught by a person who can show you the full shape and movement of each letter. In case no one is around to teach you, you can try to learn from the illustrations here.

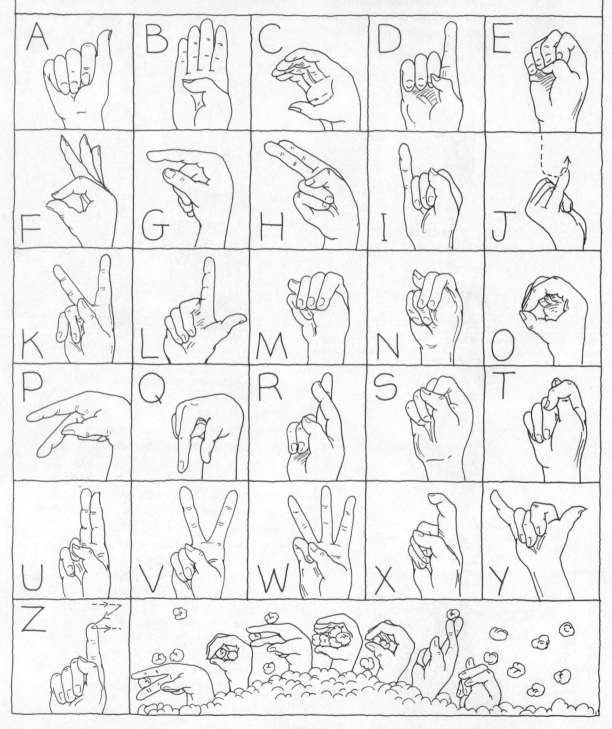

Try to fingerspell your name, your family's names, your pet's name, the name of your city, your best friend's name, the name of this book, the hardest word you can think of, a technical word such as *electrodynamometer,* the name of a place—Timbuktu, for instance.

SIGNING

Illustrated here are some of the signs used in the American Sign Language. Sign languages are not universal. Each country has its own sign language, much as each country has its own spoken language.

If you want to learn more sign language than you see here, check the public library for books on American Sign Language (ASL). Better still, see if there is someone in your school or community who uses sign language regularly and "sign up" to learn more.

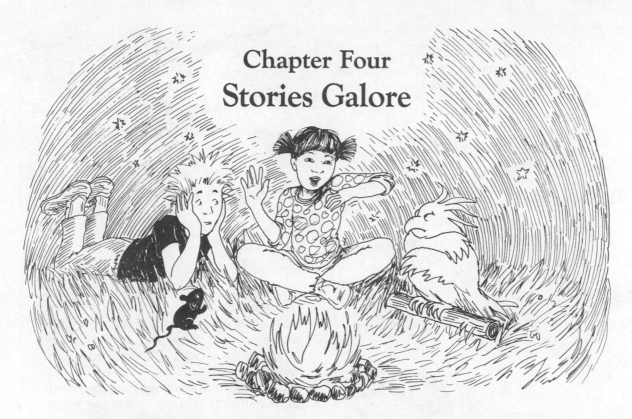

Chapter Four
Stories Galore

Everyone likes a good story. You may like it best when you're curled up on the couch reading quietly to yourself. Or perhaps you prefer a scary one, complete with sound effects, told late at night around a campfire.

There are only so many words in the English language, but we can combine them in a limitless number of ways. There are always more stories to be told. That means there is no end to how many different stories *you* can create.

Through stories we travel without airline tickets or intergalactic spaceships. You can go along on someone else's trip or create the journey yourself.

The First Stories

There's a first for everything, including stories. Though you can't find proof in any encyclopedia, the first stories were probably created by people who were trying to understand how things came to be as they are. In the process they created myths, or "maybe" stories, answering questions about how the world was created, where people came from, why the sky is blue, where the sun goes each day, and why frogs hop.

What do you think? Did frogs swallow hot, spicy green peppers and start to bounce? Or perhaps frogs compete in hurdling competitions and keep in shape with one leap after another.

Make up a few myths yourself. Feel free to add giants, superpowers, and even a dash of the impossible. After all, who does know where the sun goes each day?

The Storyteller

We're all storytellers—you, your best friend, your grandparents, the supermarket clerk, the school principal, cousin Leon, and the kid next door. How do babies tell stories? Watch one and find out.

Everyone has stories to tell, stories about anything and everything. Stories describe real happenings, such as the time your tooth fell out, the first earthquake you ever felt, or the birth of your pet kittens. Or stories can be totally imaginary.

Popular stories have long lives. Storytellers repeat them again and again, usually by popular demand. Traveling storytellers carry them across geographic and language barriers. In the telling, the story can change a bit. Here's one well-traveled story. There are at least 545 different versions of it around the world, and it's still popular. Recognize it?

Long ago, Rhodopis, an Egyptian maiden, was bathing in the Nile River, as she did every day at dawn. One day an eagle flew down and carried away her gilded sandal. Rather odd, she thought.

She would have thought the event stranger still had she seen the eagle deposit her sandal on the king's lap. Surprised himself, the king studied the sandal, finding it so impressive he decided to marry the owner if he could find her.

The royal search began. Finally, the king learned of a young woman who visited the Nile at dawn each day. He journeyed there and met the startled Rhodopis. Naturally, the sandal fit. The king rejoiced and requested her hand in marriage. They married and lived happily ever after.

You've heard this story before. In the version you have heard, the young woman's name is Cinderella and the prince falls in love with her, not with her sandal.

Now you be the storyteller. Before you get started, think about what you like when someone tells you a story. Keep those things in mind when you take over as the teller.

Pick your story: an event that really happened to you, a story you wrote, or a favorite you've read or heard. Go over the story. If it is written, read it to yourself and out loud a few times for practice. Then find your listener and tell it. Here are a few storytelling hints:

1. Your voice adds pizzazz to the sounds of words, making the story lively for your listener. Your softest voice adds mystery; a louder voice adds punch or surprise. Your audience also listens with its eyes, watching your expressions and hand gestures.

2. You are the best storytelling equipment available. Of course, you always have options to create special settings for mood. That could mean lighting a candle or telling the story inside a tent on a sleepout. What about sound effects? Is this the kind of story that works best by letting the group truly hear the sound of a door suddenly slamming (two blocks of wood hit together) or of a rainstorm (a jar of beans shaken slowly and then faster and faster)? These soundmakers add excitement to storytelling.

3. Hand puppets can tell an entire story for you. Pictures, photographs, clothing, food—these can add a special touch, smell, or sight to your story.

The Art of Observing

When you first walk into a room, what do you notice? Do the colors of the walls jump out at you, or is it the smell of baking bread you notice? In both cases, your senses are at work. You have five basic senses that serve as alarm clocks to your surroundings and help your observation skills tune into the environment: sight, sound, touch, smell, and taste.

Here's a simple quiz. Figure out which senses you would use to make better sense in each situation.

1. While you are on a bike ride, there is a faint meow that seems to be coming from overhead.

2. You hate anchovies and specifically ordered your pizza without them, but just one bite tells you the dreaded ingredient is there.

3. One night you head down a dark hall to your bedroom after watching a late show on television. A snicker forewarns you that your kid brother and his friend may be up to something. You reach for the doorknob and get a handful of a sticky gooey mess.

4. It's time to gather wood for a campfire, and you're elected to do the chore. Off you go into the woods. After about twenty absorbing minutes, with an armful of twigs and branches, you realize you aren't sure of the way back. Suddenly, a whiff of the beans your dad is cooking for dinner grabs your attention.

5. You arrive at your grandmother's house for dinner when she's frantically searching the house for her eyeglasses. You join in and are checking under the sofa, on the bookcases, by the telephone when you notice a glimmer of glass on the top of her head.

The answers to this simple quiz are in the back of the book.

44

Senses help out all the time by giving us information. Not all people have the same "sense-ability." For example, a blind person cannot depend on sight for observing, but she or he may be able to strengthen a different sense. Perhaps touch awareness or listening skills help create a fuller, more accurate sensitivity to her or his environment.

Sharpen your senses; be observant. You'll find your memory improves. As a story creator, you'll be able to dip into a pool of personal experience to enhance what you write and tell.

Pass Stories with the Gang

The "gang" might be your neighborhood group, kids from school, or your family after a hefty dinner when no one can move from the table. Distribute a piece of paper and a pen to each person. Announce that when you say "Go," each person should begin writing a story about any subject at all, whatever comes to mind. You take part too.

After two or four minutes of writing, call out "Pass." At that time each person passes his or her paper to the person on the right. Everyone writes again, this time continuing the story now in hand. After two or four minutes, call out "Pass" again; the papers move to the right, and write on. You can read as much of the entire story as you like before making additions.

Keep up the write/pass routine until the next pass would send it back to the person who started it. Before it goes "home," the last writer writes an ending and gives it a title. Call out "Pass" one last time, sending the papers home. Take turns reading them aloud. You'll hear a bit of everyone on each page.

Taking the Mystery OUT of Story Writing

Writing a story may seem like a mystery, but, without a doubt, you have a basic ingredient in your life that appears in nearly every story: conflict. The word *conflict* comes from the Greek language, and its roots mean "striking together."

Conflicts can exist inside you as internal debates about this or that. And they happen between people. Conflicts are caused by our having different needs, ideas, and values and by indecision. Even nature can cause conflict; for example, a rainstorm can interfere with plans for a picnic.

What conflicts exist in your life? Were there any in the past? Recognize any of these?

Some of the conflicts listed here take place inside you, some with other people. Think about where the following conflicts are taking place.

1. Your taste buds crave Chinese food and pizza at the same time.

2. You have plans to go to the movies with two friends who just had a big fight with each other.

3. Do your homework now and miss playing baseball, or do it later and miss your favorite TV show.

4. You feel a bit of family pressure to get your hair cut.

5. Both you and your sister want to make phone calls at the same time.

6. You found a wallet containing $175 in cash on a deserted sidewalk.

In each case, what would you do? You and a friend can separately write out how you would handle each of these situations. Compare your methods and the reasons behind them.

Don't be surprised when you find out that your life is filled with conflicts. That's true about everyone. What is interesting is how we manage them. Would you turn over the wallet and cash to the local police station? Or would you pocket the money for a new ten-speed bike? Or would you do something else?

Life without conflict seems impossible. Conflict presents challenges and makes life more exciting. It stimulates new ideas, explorations, and solutions. Conflict makes for change—some we like and some we don't.

Stories are filled with conflict because stories reflect life's events. Reading about how people handle conflict and coming up with your own solutions give you practice that carries over into your everyday life.

Think about the two following situations. Which story interests you more?

Betty caught the bus after school, just as she did every other day. The ride carried her past blooming cherry trees and the supermarket. She had homework to do that night and she wanted to call Zoe for her birthday.

OR

Karyn found a seat by herself on the bus. She needed time to think, and not about her math quiz. What to do about Judy? Her best friend was stealing from Ms. Sparks's wallet. She hardly remembered to get off at her stop. "This will be one long night," she sighed.

Betty's story is okay, but Karyn's gives you something to think about and figure out. What would *you* do?

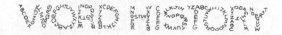

Anything Fishy About Your Ketchup?

Yup! The Chinese coined the word *ke-tsiap* to mean "pickled fish sauce." The English language kept the word and threw out the fish.

Classic Conflicts

Let's take a look at a familiar, conflict-filled story: "The Three Pigs." Three pigs (we'll call them Freddie, Sarah, and Sam) and a wolf (Max) have a classic conflict of interests: the pigs are interested in building a house; the wolf is interested in feasting on the pigs.

Freddie, Sarah, and Sam set out to build a house out of straw. Max huffs, puffs, and blows the straw all over the place. For house number two the pigs use wood, but another huff and puff results in a pile of toothpicks. The third house, made of bricks, is puff proof, and the conflict is fully resolved when Max climbs down the chimney, ending up in a pot of stew. Goodbye, Max; end of conflict.

Or is it? There were probably more conflicts in that story than ever got into print. First of all, how did the pigs ever decide which materials to use? What if Sarah wanted to go for bricks all along, but the other two insisted on straw and then wood? Conflict.

Turn the same story into a modern-day conflict. Here's the scenario: The three pigs work in construction, building houses. They are continually pestered by a wolf wearing a three-piece suit who vows to knock down their building if they don't get the proper permits.

Take any familiar story and look more closely at the conflicts. If you add one ingredient, you can change the entire conflict and its outcome. Would Little Red Riding Hood's grandmother end up in a closet if she knew karate? What if the three bears locked their door? Maybe Goldilocks would end up dining with the three pigs. And if the kiss turned the princess into a frog instead of the frog into a prince, would they live hoppily ever after?

Great Beginnings

Runners stretch before a marathon race to flex and loosen their muscles. Here's a writer's warmup.

The Five-minute Challenge

You need a timer (kitchen clocks are great), a few sheets of paper, and a pen. Set the timer for five minutes and get to writing. Keep writing as fast as you can till you hear the bell. If you get stuck, write "I'm stuck" again and again until the next idea comes. Throw all writing rules out the window. That means no pauses for spelling or paragraphs, and sloppy punctuation is permitted.

Take this challenge as many times as you want. Results are never the same. You might even hatch an idea for another writing project.

A Storehouse of Experience

Let one of these story starters trigger your memory and help you to write what really happened. Or just let your imagination roll.

1. I set out to bake a cake when . . .
2. The trip began quietly until . . .
3. If you think that's embarrassing, get a load of this.
4. As I was dozing off to sleep, I heard a . . .
5. Just as I got going on my homework, the lights . . .
6. Would you like to know about the world's best pet?
7. Absolutely no one compares with my (aunt, cousin, friend, step-brother, teacher, mom, dad, sister).

Can you imagine what it would be like to be a pencil? a car? a garbage can? a mirror? *Become the thing* and write "your" life's story. Tell about how you were born, the highs and lows of your day, and what you like to do on a free afternoon. Maybe you've heard some interesting gossip or news while working with these human beings. (If you are so inclined, turn your object's story into a comic strip.)

Alphabet Soup

You may have eaten alphabet soup and tried to put together words in your spoon before you swallowed them. With alphabet stories you feed on the alphabet to help you write a different sort of way.

One way is to pick a letter, *a*, for instance. Begin writing, using as many words as you can that begin with *a*. *An artist ate apples all afternoon.* Continue with the same letter until you run out of ideas or until you get bored, then switch to another letter, such as *l*. *Little Larry liked lemon lollipops.*

For a trickier approach to alphabet stories, make the first word begin with *a*, the second with *b*, and so on. *Alfred's bicycle cruised down Elderberry Farm.* Change the alphabet story rules anytime you like.

Back-track Story

Are you tired of writing stories from beginning to end? Create a back-track story and write the end first.

But after all that, she was too tired to eat the ice cream sundae. [Why is she so tired? What's "that"? As a back-tracker, you figure it out, maybe like this.] *The entire city gathered to celebrate her bravery.* [Back up even more.] *Never before had anyone known a twelve-year-old to catch bank robbers singlehandedly.* [Keep backing up in the story, all the way to the first line.] *Emily thought this would be a typical August morning.* [Connect the end to the beginning . . . in reverse.]

Eyes into Cameras

With care you raise the object slowly, gently, knowing any slight move could cause an explosion. Then, easing your hand over to the brown glass bowl, you tap the rim once, twice, and it happens. Oozing out of the white casing in a clear jelly followed by a river of yellow, landing on target, smack in the middle.

Have you ever heard the cracking of an egg described like that before? Turn your eyes into cameras and the paper into film. Record every second of a common event. Here are some ideas: getting up from a cushy pillow, taking out the garbage, feeding your cockatiel, unsnarling a tangle from your hair, watching popcorn pop.

Nonrepeaters

Write nonrepeaters. This story uses each word only once. Try short ones, twenty-five words in length. Go for fifty; one hundred and you're a champ! (This description of nonrepeaters has twenty-five nonrepeating words.)

Putting the Mystery INTO Story Writing

Does writing a mystery seem like a mystery? Mysteries are usually "who-did-its": someone (who) did something (what) to someone (another who). And there's the question "why?"—the reason, or motive, for the action.

The reader of the mystery may have all the information. In fact, you may really want to warn a character—don't open the door—because you know what is on the other side.

In mysteries, suspense builds as the story unfolds. Every incident moves toward the high point, the thrilling moment when the mystery is solved.

Think of mysteries that fill your life:

- The Case of the Missing Ingredients
- The Unidentified Voice on the Phone
- The Missing Homework
- The Scented Letter
- The Mysterious Box That You Open on Your Birthday
- The House That Looks Empty from the Outside but in Which You Suddenly See a Moving Figure

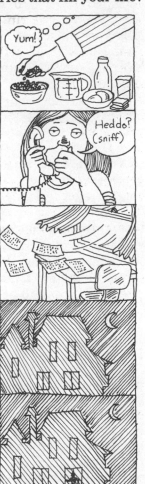

Who solves these mysteries? It can be anyone, even a trusty feline or a snoopy mutt. Whoever solves the question is usually pretty keen on detail, paying close attention to every little thing.

A private detective may solve the riddle of the broken piano, or a curious you may figure out why the flowers seem to move while the family sleeps. Some mysteries require more than one brain, following the old adage "two heads are better than one." Joint effort can produce new angles and perspectives.

Orange You a Good Detective?

Get yourself a large bag of oranges. Pick out one and look it over very carefully, noticing every imaginable detail. Return your orange to the bag, then spill all of them on the floor or table and see if you can find the one you first picked. Did you find it? Are you sure?

Practice looking at other items that you think are all alike. An almost insignificant difference can provide the clue to solving the mystery.

Clues and You

Here are the cases. You solve the mystery and write the story.

The Missing Cake

You arrive at a friend's house. As you stop to pet the family dog, your friend explains that a cake he made this afternoon is gone. You head into the kitchen and find that the refrigerator door is open. Inside, a container of milk has been knocked over. As you glance in the trash can, you see pieces of a broken dessert plate inside a crumpled paper towel.

Lurking in the Shadow

You receive a phone call from one of your friends who is calling from a telephone booth. On the way to the store on her bike, she noticed that someone in a small car was following her. When she left the store, she discovered a paper bag sitting in the basket attached to her bike. The car was nowhere to be seen.

Creaks in the Attic

Lately, before you fall asleep, you've been kept awake by what sounds like creaks in the attic. You used to spend time up there during the day a few years ago. Every now and then, when you were all alone, you "imagined" a whispering voice. Tonight your cousin is staying over. At 3:00 in the morning you're both awakened by the same creaking noises.

Any Clues About Clue?

According to Greek mythology, Theseus entered a labyrinth—an elaborate maze—searching out the monster Minotaur. He had only a thread to help him find his way. In Middle English, a thread called a *clewe* meant "a guide for Theseus to get out of the maze after killing the beast." *Clue* comes from *clewe* and still means "a guide to a puzzling situation."

Out of This World — Sci-Fi

On the barren planet Zargonia, deep in the Frod Galaxy, human forms come out from behind giant rocks. More and more forms slowly emerge from lone hiding places. Stranded for thirty-five years, these space travelers struggle to rebuild their lives and to find a way back to Earth.

One of those people is you. How did you get there, and what's going to happen next? You won't find the answers in any book. They exist in your imagination, so it's up to you to either figure out a way back to Earth or make the best of your life on Zargonia.

With science fiction you stretch your imagination to outer spaces and inner places. Sci-fi can carry you to Zargonia or pull you into the tiniest cells for conversations with mitochondria.

In the early 1900s science-fiction writers wrote about what were considered outlandish things — robots doing the work of humans and thinking computers. Space travel originated in science fiction, and the idea of a human footprint on the moon seemed preposterous except in sci-fi.

Science fiction brings life to wishful thinkers and dreamers. You remove all limits with sci-fi. What might surprise you is that much of what is written in current science fiction will come to pass within your lifetime.

Meanwhile, back on Zargonia, what about a shrinking school? or the surprise you felt when the first robot family moved into the house next door? or when you fall into a time warp and find yourself in the year 1785? Science fiction — off you go.

Word Pool

Imagine a swimming pool filled with words. Dive in and bring out a handful with you. Start with an even dozen. Write a story and use each of the words in it. Share your word pool with one of your friends. If you both start with the same words, do you get the same results?

To make a word pool, get a box, small pieces of paper, and a pen. Write a word on each piece and place them in the box. Anytime you like, dig in and get words to use in your story.

Another way to fill your pool is to gather old magazines, then cut out words and put them in your pool.

WORD HISTORY

Tulips Grow in Turkey

At least this one did. Although you may imagine fields of *tulips* growing in Holland, the word is Turkish for *turban* and refers to the flower's shape. Any turbans in your garden?

Chapter Five
You, Too, Are a Poet

You are a poet, even if you have never written a poem. That's because you *could* write 1, 2, 683, or more. Why would you write a poem? There are many possible reasons—to entertain, to amuse, to spill out the secrets from your heart, as food for thought, to tell a story, or just because you feel like it.

If you already like poetry, this chapter has plenty to occupy you. If you haven't been around poems very much, here's your chance to get familiar. If you think you don't like poetry, look again and try a few as you go. You may find pleasant poetry surprises along the way. Let the poet inside come out.

Is This a Poem?

This is it—your chance to choose poems from nonpoems. Which are, and which are not?

I once knew a poem very well
The words were as clear as a bell
    It began with a rhyme
    And it rhymed all the time
And this is that poem, could you tell?

A fly crossed
in   f
                            r
                            o
                            n
                            t
of my   n
        o
        s
        e
to   day I tried to
        k
         e e
            p
t
r   a c k
of   it   bu t
it
    flew
a   w a   y

Clouds slip by
painting pictures in
the early morning.

Which should I have
for breakfast,
clouds or cereal ?

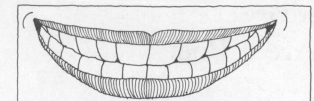

When you smile
Make it stretch a mile
With Miles of Smiles Toothpaste!
Makes your teeth bright
And glow in the night
Use Miles of Smiles Toothpaste!

First mix eggs, milk
Let butter soften
Only the finest ingredients
Wait while it bakes, soon to
Eat delicious cake. Oh! Was that the
Right flower?

After you read the following questions, go back and look over the poems. Do they all look the same? Do they all rhyme? Do any tell a story? Are they fun or serious? Are they all poems? The answers to these questions are up to you. There aren't any right answers.

"Three Blind Mice" is *not* a poem!

Yep. 'Fraid so.

What is a poem? A poem may be one of the most difficult things in the world to describe since it can be many different things all at the same time. One thing is for certain: People make poems.

People create poetry to express personal feelings, thoughts, ideas, and especially to let out strong beliefs or passions. Poems also can be strictly for fun. As a poet, or poem creator, you can ignore rules for sentences, punctuation, capital letters, spelling, you name it, or you can follow them. Your poems can use words, shapes, and images; they may rhyme, but they don't have to. If you set a poem to music, you have a song, and you know plenty of those.

Making poetry is old business; it has been going on for thousands of years. A poem written over 4,000 years ago has been found, and the writer's name was still attached to it—Enheduanna, daughter of a king and a moon priestess. Many of her poems address goddesses as friends. She asks them for help.

O my lady, on hearing your sound,
hills and flatlands bow.
When we come before you,
terrified, shuddering in your stormy
  clear light
we receive justice.

In the 4,000 years since Enheduanna wrote her poems, millions of poems have been written in all sorts of ways. Rules, if any, are decided by the poet; and in this case, that's you.

All in Your Name

To join the poetry bandwagon, you need a piece of paper, a pen, and your name. Write your name along the paper's left side margin, one letter per line. These letters instantly become the first letter of the first word on each line of your poem. You add the rest.

If your name is Leslie, your first line begins with a word starting with *L*, and since you and music are inseparable, that's part of your poem.

L et the music play!
E ach note a
S ong. Do you
L ove to sing
I n the shower when
E veryone's gone?

Use your first, middle, and last names and stretch the full length of the paper. Any birthdays coming up? Name poems make great gifts.

Name poems can be written tandem, that's with two people. Trade off on writing lines. Do your own names, then write them for friends and family. How about a name poem for your pet turtle, Skipperdee?

A School for Dolls

Do students look like dolls, sitting quietly? At one time maybe they did. The word *pupil* came from the Latin word *pupilla*, meaning "a little doll."

Take a close look into a friend's eye and you'll see your own reflection. The Romans named the *pupil* in the eye for the miniature picture of ourselves that is reflected there.

Say Hi to Haiku

Haiku (pronounced HIGH-koo) are short poems with a particular rhythm and form. Haiku describe a scene in nature, capturing a special moment filled with emotion. They rarely rhyme.

Haiku originated long ago in Japan as part of a contest. Competitors, given the first three lines of a poem, had to add two more. If you created the best lines, you won. The name *haiku* comes from this contest—*hokku,* meaning "starting verse."

So what's a haiku these days? Read this one by the Japanese poet Boncho and figure it out.

The red sun sinks low
Beyond a dead tree clutching
An old eagle's nest

Here is another haiku; this one is by Kikaku.

Poor crying cricket,
perhaps your little husband
was caught by our cat.

You may have already figured out how many lines make up a haiku: three. Do the number of words per line seem to matter? Check the two haiku you just read. How many words are in each line? Are they the same? How about the number of syllables in each line?

A syllable is a sound; one or more of them make up words. Some words have one syllable: me, toy, store, you. Words can have two syllables: win-dow, base-ball. *Syllable* has three syl-la-bles, and so does pop-si-cle. How many syllables are in your name?

How many syllables are in each of these words: over, Timbuktu, monkey, California, octogenarian, particular, stove. A short word can have more syllables than a long one. Compare *Ohio* with *birthday.*

Take another look at the haiku. Count the number of syllables in each line. If you discovered that the first line has five syllables, the second line seven, and the last one five again, you solved the riddle of the syllables in haiku, 5-7-5.

What If They Had Been Called Castles?

They weren't. Seeds from Armenia were planted and cultivated at Castle Cantaloupo in Ancona, Italy. Which fruit was that?

What are haiku about? Generally speaking, haiku have some reference to or connection with nature. Seasons, animals, and life cycles appear in haiku along with the writer's emotions.

Are you ready to try one? Situate yourself in a scenic spot such as a backyard, a park, a neighborhood junkyard, near a window, or close to a pet. To get started, forget the syllables and write three lines describing your setting or what you're watching. Then go back and count syllables.

You can always lengthen or shorten a line later. It is important to keep your idea and feelings in the poem just the way you want them. The 5-7-5 syllable arrangement is a guide, not a rule.

With haiku you don't have to finish your thought. It's a moment in time, part of a picture. Let the reader fill in the rest.

Carry a haiku notebook for when the mood arises. Use your own drawings, photographs, or scenic pictures from magazines to inspire you to write haiku. Give some as gifts.

It is fun to write haiku with a friend or two. Each person contributes one line to the poem. Work together to make the syllable adjustments.

I'm in the Mood for . . .

Whatever mood you're in, that's a fine mood for writing poetry. Quiet? Take paper and pen or a poetry notebook to a special private place and spend a few moments listening to the sounds of quiet: your breathing, heartbeat, crickets, refrigerator hmmmm. How do you feel being alone and just where you are? When you're ready, write it down.

Musical? Sprawling out on the carpet with your favorite music playing, write a poem as the musical notes travel from your head to your toes. Listening to some not-so-familiar music? What kind of poem does it inspire?

Sad? Poetry can be a fine friend when no one else is available.

Celebrating? A poem of joy and hurrah can be just the thing. Write one as you celebrate. (Keep it around to read on a not-so-terrific day.)

Noisy? With friends or alone, let the clamor and spirit fill each wild, noisy, smashing word.

Poems You Can't Write Alone

Why not alone? They're collaborative poems, and by the very nature of the word *collaborative,* they involve two or more people. Gather a few friends together and get started.

You will need paper strips 1 to 2 inches wide and about 6 inches long, a long sheet of paper, tape, and pens.

Give strips of paper and pens to everyone. Instruct each person to write one phrase or sentence on the paper that includes a color, an animal, and a place.

When everyone is done, collect the strips and shuffle them together. Next, tape each strip on the long sheet, one under the other. Then read the poem.

Collaborative poems can be written about any subject at all. Distribute strips of paper again; this time each person writes two phrases on his or her piece of paper. Begin the first line with "I used to be . . ." Begin the second line with "But now I am . . ." Collect and mount the strips before you read the results.

Make a wall full of collaborative poetry, and speaking of a wall full, try a poetry art wall bonanza. Get a large sheet of butcher paper, a group of people, and colored marking pens. Spread the paper out on the floor or on a huge table and gather around all sides. Spend the first ten minutes drawing whatever comes to mind; then spend the next five minutes writing poems on the same sheet. Work alone or in pairs. Switch back and forth from art to poems until the paper is a "wallfull."

A Hairy Cat

Do you have one? It's probably just an old caterpillar. Now don't get insulted. The word *caterpillar* comes from an old French word, *chatepelose,* meaning "hairy cat."

Ode to My Toothbrush

An ode is a kind of poem dedicated to a person, place, or thing. You write each word with that in mind. To rhyme or not to rhyme is up to you.

An ode can be a passionate plea to your true love for a promise of hand and heart ("My Love, My Love, What Shall I Do?"). Odes can also express gratitude to your frying pan for making the best grilled cheese sandwiches on the block ("Hey, Pan, You're the Best"). In other words, odes can be quite serious or just the opposite.

Just so you get the idea, here's an ode to an object we can all appreciate.

Toothbrush, oh, Toothbrush
You fit my hand so well
  Each morn and night
  We brush just right
My teeth glow, can't you tell?

Toothbrush, my Toothbrush
With bristles standing tall
  Your handle pink
  Stays by the sink
In your holder on the wall.

Toothbrush, old Toothbrush
Like an old familiar song
  I hate to say
  Today's the day
I have a new one now, So Long!

Pick something or someone you appreciate and say so in an ode. You can write odes to long-lost friends; Hackensack, New Jersey; or a baseball bat.

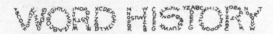

Poems for All Occasions

Did something special just happen? Did someone you know have a birthday? a baby? graduate from high school? learn how to read? Or maybe someone you know is stuck in bed with a rotten cold. Whatever the occasion, you can add something special with a personalized poem.

Personal poems fit the occasion and the person like absolutely nothing you could buy. You give the personal touch.

For starters, take a favorite poem or song. Make a few changes in it so it is about the person and the special event.

Twinkle, twinkle, my big sis,
How I wonder about this:
On a morning in July,
You gave birth to this wee guy.

Write it out; then give a private reading or singing. Try composing a medley of tunes for a party and having all the guests sing along.

Is That a Kangaroo? I Don't Know

When the British Captain Cook landed in Australia and saw the hopping marsupial, he asked, "What is that called?" A native Australian replied in his language, "I don't know," which sounded to Captain Cook like *kangaroo*. Will a kangaroo ever know what it is?

Chapter Six
Meet the Press

If you are curious about what's happening in your neighborhood, community, or around the world and have an "itch" to find out news and information, how can you do it? Many methods have been used. Runners among the Incas in South America carried news via a 3,000-mile network in just five days. "Talking" drums spread the news of coming rain, travelers, celebrations, war, and births in Mandingo country in western Africa. Traveling land caravans, ships, and aircraft have carried inhabitants of our shrinking planet (like you) around the globe to collect information.

Today you don't have to run several thousand miles or sail to distant lands for current news. You can find a bundle of news on your doorstep each morning or at the corner store: newspapers. Now is your chance to meet the press. Once you've met it, you may want to start your own.

The Five Ws

What are the five Ws? A singing group, perhaps? Check your newspaper and you'll find the five Ws all over the place. Whenever newspaper reporters cover a story, they make sure the five Ws are included. The five Ws contain nineteen letters when added together, and each of the five Ws has *wh* as its first two letters. Even when you know what the five Ws are, you're still missing an important ingredient of most newspaper articles. Make your guesses now or never because the next paragraph reveals the identity of the five Ws.

Here they are: who, what, when, where, why.

As a reporter, you're out to find the facts, the answers to who did what, when and where did it happen, and why did it take place at all? You must try to find the best, most reliable source for the information. In addition, you have one more ingredient to discover: How did it occur? Now that you have a head full of the five Ws and an H, you are ready to head out to find the news. Read the following articles. Did the reporter leave out anything?

FABULOUS GAME FRIDAY

What a game! The Cougars played their rivals, the Comets, at the coliseum. A sellout crowd gathered to watch one of the nation's two top teams become the champion.

Both teams played well. On the sidelines, Coach Al Crispi said, "You're watching basketball at its best!"

When the game was over, the audience left slowly, with cheers for the winning team echoing in their ears.

VOLCANO ERUPTS
FIREFIGHTERS SAVE LIVES

At 3:00 A.M. a previously inactive volcano erupted. The sound was heard as far away as 2 miles. The explosion in the volcano's interior released a smoke cloud that was visible for 250 miles. Within twelve minutes a stream of hot lava poured down the northern wall of the crater.

Firefighters arrived on the scene at 3:30 A.M. They advised residents in neighboring farmhouses of evacuation procedures and provided assistance. Their quick movement saved 165 people from the fire that engulfed the area by 4:35 A.M.

A Little Battle on the Board

Backgammon—that's Welsh for "little battle," a popular board game supposedly created by an Indian man, Qaflan. The game is designed to represent the solar year: twenty-four points on the board for the hours in the day; thirty moving pieces for the average number of days in a month; two dice, one for night and one for day; and the opposite sides on each die add up to seven, for the number of days of the week.

YOUNGEST SCIENTISTS EVER
RECEIVE NATIONAL AWARDS

Three junior high students were given the Science for Us awards by the Scientists for a Better Tomorrow organization.

At a banquet held November 28 in New York City, Professor Ellis congratulated Heidi Ross, Laura Shira, and Ricardo Moravi for "their brilliant achievements. They have opened new doors with their discoveries. Youth will lead the way to a safer future."

Each young person will receive a check for $500 and a plaque listing her or his accomplishment.

Rewrite each of these articles and fill in the missing information. Then write your own news article. Cover an election or sports event at your school. Or are there any neighborhood projects you can write about?

Fact or Opinion?

Compare the following three newspaper articles. Do you notice some differences?

1

CITY MAY CLOSE LIBRARY

Today's city council meeting focused on closing the central library. Council member Kelsaw made a brief statement following the meeting, "The building is old. The books can be distributed to other locations. A local construction company has offered a large sum of money for the property, and with our current budget problems, we can use all the money we can get."

Since the library is located in her district, council member Dyson expressed her concern, "This proposal is an outrage! The library serves a large population, and I will not permit this unnecessary loss to our community."

Public comment can be heard on October 17 at the city hall at 10:00 A.M.

2

LIBRARY CLOSING

It's about time. I never liked the downtown library, and now council member Kelsaw has a plan to close it. He submitted the proposal today, and I hope it passes.

Council member Dyson says she'll fight it, but I hope she fails. Personally I don't use any library. If they closed them all, the city would save a lot of money.

Go to the city hall October 17 at 10:00 A.M. and tell the council members that you think they should close the library.

3

SOMETHING CONCERNING THE LIBRARY

Something is happening with the library downtown. One member of the council wants to close it, and another member wants to keep it open. There's a meeting sometime so the public can be heard. It might be before the end of this month, or maybe it is next month.

The first article gives you the facts, straight and clear. You don't learn many facts in the second one, and the third one tells even fewer. A newspaper reporter has a responsibility to the readers: Present reliable information as clearly as possible. By providing just the facts, you allow the readers to draw their own conclusions and decide what they think about what's happening in the news. Although it's natural for every writer to have an opinion about a subject, that opinion doesn't belong in a news article.

68

What about the reporter's personal opinions? They're kept in a section that is clearly marked "Editorials." Or you may see an individual article labeled "Commentary." Those terms mean "this is filled with personal opinion."

Despite the best possible efforts, personal opinion can and does slip into news articles. Sometimes an entire newspaper will present one particular viewpoint instead of reporting several different perspectives. As you read the newspaper, keep an eye out for opinions. As *you* write newspaper articles, what will you do with your opinions?

All the News

The *New York Times* began using the motto "All the News That's Fit to Print" on October 25, 1896. The paper sponsored a contest, offering $100 for a better motto. Out of 20,000 entries one winner emerged: "All the World's News, But Not a School for Scandal." Still, the *New York Times* kept its old motto.

Under the Big Top

Under the Big Top, performing in the rings, are elephants, clowns, acrobats, tightrope walkers, and lion tamers. The Greek word *kirkos,* meaning "ring" or "circle," became *circus* in Latin, and the word is still going around.

Letter to the Editor

One part of the newspaper is reserved for opinion; it is the editorial section and is named for the editor-in-chief, who oversees everything printed in the newspaper.

Find the editorial section in a daily newspaper. It probably includes articles expressing a point of view taken by the newspaper's editorial staff, articles written by individuals stating personal opinions, and letters from readers saying what they think about current issues in the news. Anyone can write letters to the editor of the newspaper. A special staff selects which ones will be printed.

Have you read the editorial section in your newspaper? Which current issues are being covered? Do these issues affect your community, your state, the entire United States, or the entire world? Do you agree with the point of view expressed? Write your reaction in the form of a letter to the editor.

Dear Editor,

I'm a sixth-grade student at Round Valley Elementary School. I was glad to read your recent editorial "Bus Fares Too High." After school I take a bus to my piano lesson and another one home. A hike in fares would take a big bite out of my allowance, which helps to pay for my piano lessons.
Signed, Eileen

Of course, you can disagree with the editorial commentary.

Dear Editor,

You printed an article stating that young people do not care about elderly people. We think you're wrong! Many kids care and want to be involved in programs for the elderly. If more community groups had kids on planning committees, we could come up with great ideas about how to help. On our own we lack money and public support but not interest and energy.
Signed, Selena, Darryl, and Kim

Which issues concern you? Send your reactions to your local newspaper.

Fabulous Funnies

If you read the funny pages first, you aren't alone. Newspaper publishers know that many readers head straight for the funnies before anything else. Papers run assorted cartoon strips since you like one kind and your friend may like another. You'll find comics of different lengths, and some have ongoing stories, from intergalactic battles to soap operas. There are talking animals, cave people listening to radios, and characters that never age. Charlie Brown has been the same age since "Peanuts" was first printed in 1950.

The first regular comic section appeared in the New York *World* in 1889; it was called "Hogan's Alley." Cartoons have been appearing ever since. Not all newspapers carry comics, but family newspapers usually do.

You can make your own funnies. In the following cartoon the characters didn't quite get their words out. As the cartoonist, what would you have them say? Get a piece of paper and write out several possibilities.

This cartoon is just the opposite—all words and no characters. Who's carrying on the conversation? Animals? People? Talking table lamps? Does the meaning of the words change depending on who or what is doing the talking?

Many cartoonists model stories on their own experiences. Start your own cartoon strip. You can even have the starring role.

Work on paper to develop your main figure. Stick drawings are just fine. Think of a place where you were today. Did something happen that you can use? Draw four squares and sketch a simple setting. Put your character in it. Then look again. What are the words you want your character to say?

Plenty of Advice

Do you need some advice on pet care, your bridge game, what to wear, family matters, legal issues, money, or how to cure a sore throat? Newspapers print advice columns on a variety of topics.

What kind of advice could you get from your local paper if you wrote a letter asking for it? Look through a newspaper. All you have to do is send in your question.

What kind of advice can you give? Pick one of your specialties or make a general "Ask a Kid" column. Friends and family can send you questions. Write out your answers and make enough copies to pass around.

Your Own Newspaper

Now that you've analyzed what makes a newspaper work, it's time to start your own newspaper and to hit the presses.

The Family Press

Create a family newspaper every few months. As editor, you can make sure your "staff of reporters" meets the printing deadlines by contributing articles. Send copies to relatives and friends. It is a great way to stay in touch.

Neighborhood Gazette

Gather your friends and start a neighborhood newspaper. There are plenty of jobs for all of you. Here is a list of what might need to be done.

Editor: oversees the entire job, helping out wherever needed. Also reviews all articles.

Reporters: gather the news and write the articles, for example, an interview with a new kid in the neighborhood, plans for a community picnic and softball game, information about the antigraffiti efforts of local merchants, coverage of a bicycle inspection station set up locally for safety checks. (Every member of the newspaper staff can make valuable suggestions about stories to cover and could even share in the writing.)

Columnists: write ongoing columns that give advice, for example, "How to Make Friends and Keep Them," or that give information about food, such as, "This Week's Nutritious, Delicious Snack."

Ad manager: finds local businesses that want to buy newspaper space for advertisements or families that want to put in a notice about an upcoming garage sale.

Layout artist: gathers the articles, ads, and columns and figures out how they will fit together to form the pages of the newspaper.

Printer: receives the newspaper when it is all ready to be printed and gets the copies made (the printer may be the person who also does the layout). Check your neighborhood for printing resources; perhaps a local copying business would give you a discount in exchange for advertising space.

Subscription manager: sells single copies or a series to friends, families, and local residents.

Each neighborhood gazette is different. Undoubtedly you'll come up with your own tasks and the best way to get the job done.

A What-If? Newspaper

What if you lived in the medieval days of mythical Camelot? As Royal Newspaper Editor, you gather a trusty staff of friends to compile articles on the royal weather report; new rust-proof suits of armor; who stole the tarts baked by the queen of hearts, including the queen's recipe; Dear Merlin, an advice column on magic; come ye sports fans to the world series of jousting. You can make a "What If?" newspaper about any period of time—past, present, or future.

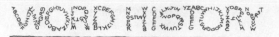

His Name Lives in a Tree

The largest and tallest living thing on earth is named after an American Indian leader. In the early 1800s Sequoyah developed a written alphabet for the Cherokee language and began the first Cherokee newspaper. The redwood tree is named in his honor.

A Free Press?

On September 25, 1690, when thirteen British colonies stretched along the Atlantic Ocean, an Englishman living in Boston printed the first newspaper in the Western Hemisphere: *Publick Occurrances Both Foreign and Domestick*. The first issue had about 5,300 words printed on three sides of four notebook-size sheets of paper. The publisher, Ben Harris, left the fourth side of the paper blank. He wanted people to write in their own news before giving the paper to other readers.

No one had a chance to add news. The government objected to Ben's articles, stopped the presses, and confiscated all the issues that could be found. Back in those days, the government controlled newspapers. Government control continued until the public said, "No! We want to know *all* the news, not just what you want us to know." A new standard was established—a free press.

What does a free press mean to you? A free press provides variety in newspapers, allowing for differing opinions and choices of subject matter. Newspaper reporters can keep their information sources confidential. In the process of investigating a story, a reporter may uncover criminal activity by a government official, for example, and print that information without the fear of being jailed. Newspapers can criticize government policies openly, without being closed down as Ben Harris's press was.

Every newspaper is responsible for documenting information accurately, for being certain resources are reliable. Reporters can't guess at news; each item has to be carefully investigated before it is printed. Otherwise, the newspaper may lose its credibility. What would you think of an article like the following one.

WRISTWATCH STOLEN

On Wednesday, March 22, Barbara said that Alan told David how Marsha heard from Laurie all about Alice's stolen wristwatch. The theft occurred either in the school gym, according to Marsha, or on the bus, according to Alan. Barbara said the watch cost a great deal, but Laurie said Alice paid just a few dollars for it.

Newspapers can't base their stories on rumors or gossip. Reliable reporting makes a free press worthwhile, and a free press is an extremely important part of our society.

In each country around the world, the government establishes standards for its press—will it be a free press or will it be subject to government review? Investigate the standards in other countries, for example, Mexico, Chile, England, Greece, Russia, India, China. Would you be willing to trade standards with any of those countries?

There Really Is a Googol

No kidding! When American mathematician Edward Kasner was trying to think of a word to name the number 1 followed by one hundred zeros, he asked his nine-year-old nephew, Milton Sirotta, for a suggestion. "A *googol*," he said. And that's what we call it.

1,000,000,000,000,000,000,000,000,000,000,000,000,...

Chapter Seven
The Play's the Thing

Anytime you stalk wild animals in the backyard or soar through space, you create theater. Alone in the living room, you pretend to sing the hit song on the radio: again, theater. Theater and make-believe go together. You can create any time and any place; you can become any person you choose. The story line may be fact or completely made up. With theater, just about anything goes.

Silent Plays

Can there be a play without a sound, without a hint of noise? Can you create a mood, tell a story, and captivate a person if your mouth is sealed shut? More than likely, yes. The silent play of *pantomime* works in just this way. Get your friends together and give it a try!

Take a Walk

Any number of people will do. One person is the caller; the rest are walkers. As the walkers walk, the caller calls out descriptions of the imaginary setting and conditions that could affect movement. Here are some things the caller might say: "You're walking in a meadow of flowers; suddenly, you're in a blackberry patch with thorns sticking out everywhere; no more thorns, now you're in mud up to your ankles, and it's rising to your knees; the mud's gone; it has turned to water and it's waist high; the water disappears; now back to the meadow, a meadow full of raw eggs, and don't step on any of them; okay, step on a few eggs." The walk can last as long as you like, carrying you up mountains and over hot coals. And not a word.

Who's on First?

Stage a silent, slow-motion baseball game, without a baseball, bat, or catcher's mitt. Let the pitcher warm up on the mound and toss a curve ball to the batter. Strike! The next pitch is a ground hit. Was everyone able to keep an eye on the ball? It's fine to make agreements about where the ball will go, base hits, and home runs. Batter up!

At the Bus Stop

Four strangers are at a bus stop. Who are they? If not a word is exchanged, can you tell which person is a banker? a musician? a tap dancer? a student? What if a bus passes by without stopping? All of you try to stare at the imaginary bus. Does everyone's head move at the same time? Try it, it's tricky.

Repeat the scene with a different group of characters on the bench. Invent your own character. The watchers can guess who you are when you're done.

Invisible Clay

Gather your friends and sit in a circle. Bring out your box of invisible clay. Take out a large chunk, roll it into a ball, work it until it's soft, then mold it into something useful, such as a telescope. Once it's made, use it. Pass it to the person on your left. If she or he can use it properly, which means she or he knows what it is, let her or him remold the clay into something else, such as a pair of glasses—the kind for drinking or the ones you see through. Keep the clay circulating around the group. Mold it, use it, pass it on.

Action

Write a play without words—only give directions of what the characters do. Here's one:

Drew enters the living room and takes a look around. No one is there. He picks up a book, sinks into the couch, and begins to read. Within moments he's fast asleep.

While he sleeps, eight friends enter the room, carrying decorations for Drew's surprise party. There are all kinds of noisy accidents, with people bumping into the couch. Drew sleeps on. Finally, the room is set; a whispered "Surprise!" awakens Drew, and the party begins.

Think of other silent places—a library, a movie theater, or an elevator. Write your silent play and get your friends to stage it.

Show Me a Story

Pick up a story you wrote, a dream you had last night, a fantasy for the future, or one of your all-time favorites. Be the storyteller while a group of your friends enacts the story as you tell it. They role-play everything you describe—the wind, trees, cat, door, clock, and people. Also, they carry out the actions. Try acting out the following paragraph.

The tree plucked an apple from its own branch and offered it to Robin. She waved goodby as the tree walked away. This is a strange place, she thought.

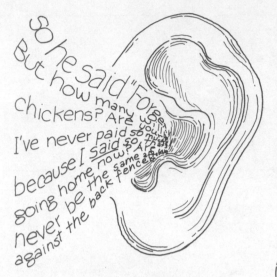

"She left town two months ago, and I haven't heard a . . ."

". . . with my blue suit, this tie is a knockout!"

"Hurry, the movie starts in twelve minutes."

Use these lines to write skits. Write one in which no one is listening to anyone. Then write a scene with characters paying attention to each other. Write any kind of scene you like, using as many of the lines that you recorded as you can.

Listen Up

Conversation between you and others includes two important parts: the sounds and the silences. Listen to people talk. Do they always use complete sentences? Do they always finish what they are saying? Do they ever interrupt each other? Are they always talking about the same thing? Are they listening to each other? Do the silences carry messages?

Get a note pad and a pen. Situate yourself in a market, on a bus, in a restaurant, or in your living room. Listen. Write down bits and pieces of conversations.

Dialogue-ing Along

What this one says to that one and that one says back is known as dialogue. When you write a play, you create the sounds and silences of what your characters say: dialogue.

Mark: Oh, come on, Theresa. You'll have another chance at winning the tournament.

Theresa: After today I may never compete again.

Mark: You're a winner, and don't forget it!

Theresa: [You fill in her response.]

Words can go back and forth as long as the playwright desires. Silences also communicate messages, often just as effectively as words do.

Jon: Hey, Fred, be a sport and pass me the newspaper.

[Fred stays seated, arms folded, staring straight ahead.]

Jon: Fred, are you still angry about yesterday?

[Fred gazes up at the ceiling and taps his foot.]

A silence can be filled with action or be absolutely quiet and continue to convey important information about what's happening on stage.

Here's your chance to be a playwright. One character's dialogue is provided. You fill in the sound or silence of response.

Scene One:

This scene takes place at John's house during an afternoon game of chess.

John: I'm glad you made that move.

Chris: [Sound or silence?]

John: This game will not last much longer.

Chris: [Your choice!]

John: Wait a minute, I didn't see that!

Chris: [Your reaction?]

John: I can't believe it

Chris: [Any last words?]

Scene Two:

This scene takes place at the beach on a hot, sunny day.

Janelle: If I stay here much longer, I may get cooked.

Lyn:

Janelle: Did you hear me?

Lyn:

Janelle: Maybe a swim is a good idea, want to come?

Lyn:

Janelle: Hey, look, everyone is running out of the water!

Lyn:

Scene Three:

Traveling in a car.

Carol: Can't you move over?

Phillip:

Carol: I'm really not interested in your book.

Phillip:

Carol: Hey, that's a photograph of the building we just passed.

Phillip:

You've been a participant in dialogue for many years. To write dialogue, you draw from your own experience and use your natural ability to imagine. If you need help getting your imagination outside yourself, try the chair technique. Gather as many chairs as there are characters in your play. Label the chairs with the characters' names if you like, then as you create the dialogue, you get up and move to the chair of the person who is going to speak.

From Thelma's chair: This visit is such a pleasant surprise!

From Willie's chair: I meant to come as soon as I heard.

From Thelma's chair: Have the rumors spread so quickly?

From Willie's chair: It's all over town. I heard it at the drugstore.

You will eventually develop your own best way for writing dialogue. Try experimenting with different approaches to stimulate new ideas.

The Thing's the Play

Write a play that brings objects, or things, to life. Describe your place, or setting, and imagine.

A scene:

A kitchen table with a large fruit bowl containing a banana, lemon, apple, pear, and kiwi.

Banana: Another day in a fruit bowl.

Pear: Life used to be a bowl of cherries.

Kiwi: I'm not ripe; I'll be around for a few days.

Apple: Not me. An apple a day keeps the doctor away, you know. I'm a goner.

What would Lemon say?

You can finish this dialogue and write other still-life plays. What about stuffed animals? living room furniture? piano keys? plants in a window box? If only they could talk.

To stage your play, you can make a cardboard cutout of each object, like a cartoon come to life. Your friends could play the roles by wearing appropriate costumes of a sign to identify the object.

The Meeting

What if you could spend fifteen minutes with anyone who ever lived? Whom would you pick? What would happen? Get a few pieces of paper and a pen and make it happen in a play. Enter a time machine, flip the switch, and off you go to converse with your favorite heroes, heroines, writers, and sports stars.

If you decided to meet Harriet Tubman, who led slaves into freedom, you might write:

Me: You are very brave to risk your life the way you do to save the lives of other slaves.

H.T.: It frightens me more to think about what will happen to my family and friends if they remain slaves than it does to keep the underground railroad in operation.

Get a few friends to write their own special meetings. Take turns acting out the parts.

83

Characters in a Box

Get a stack of three-by-five index cards and an old shoebox. Write a character's name and five things about that character on each card.

Gather a group of friends and give each person a card. Each person becomes that character during an instant show. As a group, decide where the setting is (on a baseball diamond, at a museum, in a swimming pool). Do these characters know each other, or did they just meet? Are any of them related?

Situate yourselves around a table, where each person has paper and a pen. Begin talking as these characters. Write down the lines that are said. If there aren't any speedy writers in the bunch, you can tape-record the lines and write them up later as a collectively created play.

Angie: lots of energy, talks nonstop, captain of the softball team, has kid brother with her most of the time.

You add one.

Leo: studies too much, makes great pizza, wants to be an actor.

You add two more.

A Radio Show

Before television brought us pictures, millions of radio sets brought weekly plays into our homes. "The Lone Ranger," "Gunsmoke," "Dragnet," "Burns and Allen," "Our Miss Brooks," "Life with Riley," "Space Patrol," and "Captain Midnight" were radio shows. Many became TV shows in the 1950s. In the 1980s *Star Wars* fans tuned in their radios to hear radio versions of Darth Vader and Princess Leia.

Tune in to a radio play. You hear what's happening, and your mind's eye creates the picture. You can write one yourself.

Start your own home radio station. Choose call letters, four letters to name your station. Station names start with the letter *K* or *W*—K for locations west of the Mississippi River, and W for places east of there. Your call letters can even sound like or spell a word, such as KUTE or WILD.

Plan a broadcast and write your script. You can include the following items.

News report: "Good evening. This is Helene, bringing you the local update. At 4:15 this afternoon a child was reunited with her parents."

Weather forecast: "If you have plans for a picnic tomorrow, I have good news. We predict that tomorrow will be warm and sunny."

Advertisements: "Thirsty? Reach for a tall glass of fresh orange juice."

Sports: "The scores are in. On the courts today, Lisa won the city tennis championship."

Feature: "Tonight we bring you the first episode of [*sound of dog howling*] 'Mystery at Midnight' [*sound of door slamming*]. Descend the creaking steps [*sound of footsteps*] into Dr. Higano's basement, where early in the morning she works with her assistant Julian."

Dr. H.: Julian [*sound of water pouring into a jar*], the experiment works!

Julian: Amazing, after all these years.

Dr. H.: But is the world ready for this? [*sound of doorbell*] Who could that be at this time of the morning?

Who is at the door? What kind of experiment must the world be ready for? Continue the episode to its thrilling conclusion. After you have written the script, get your sound-effects equipment together. Give a live reading or make a tape. You can play all the parts, or you can include your friends.

Setting the Stage

In a play you create a situation with your written words and characters. Something takes place that draws the imagination of the audience into the life onstage. That's the magic of the play.

Sometimes you may want to create a visual environment for your players. You can choose not to leave so much to the imagination. Collect some furniture or make some trees and buildings, for example, and before you know it you have *set the stage*.

Do you want to create a *backdrop* that shows where your play is taking place? You'll need the following materials: drawing paper and pens; a few old sheets, one per scene; marking pens; water-soluble paints; paint brushes; styrofoam cups; five long pieces of wood; a hammer and nails; and a heavy-duty stapler.

1. Decide what your scenes will be — neighborhood street, forest, kitchen — and sketch drawings on paper. Make your drawings simple, especially on your first try as a set designer.

2. Stretch out a sheet on a flat surface. Use the marking pen to outline your sketch on the sheet.

3. Prepare to paint. It's easier to handle paint if you pour each color as you're using it into a styrofoam cup. Keep the paint can covered. Paint your drawing. Be sure to read the directions on the paint can.

4. Drying time for the sheets will vary. Allow several hours.

5. Use the wood to construct a giant easel as a frame to hold the sheets.

6. After the sheets are dry and the easel has been built, it's time to put them together. If you have more than one sheet, get the one that will be used *last* in your show. Staple it on the cross piece of the easel. Continue stapling the sheets in the reverse order that they will be used. The top sheet will then be your opening scene.

7. To change the scene during the play, flip a sheet. Save old scenes for future productions.

THE GIANT EASEL

This can be built to whatever size you need. Check dimensions at a local lumber yard.

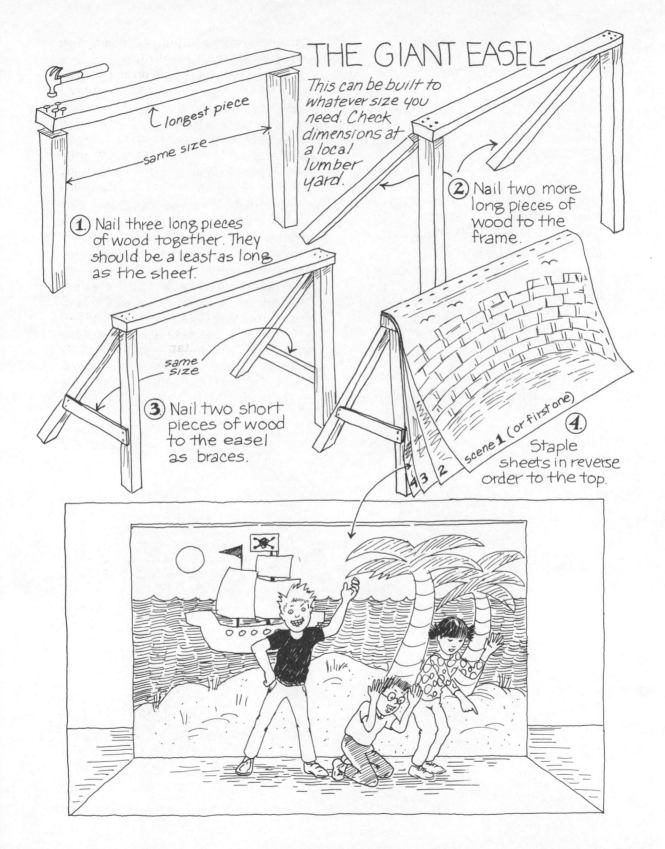

longest piece

same size

1. Nail three long pieces of wood together. They should be a least as long as the sheet.

2. Nail two more long pieces of wood to the frame.

same size

3. Nail two short pieces of wood to the easel as braces.

scene **1** (or first one)

4 3 2

4. Staple sheets in reverse order to the top.

cardboard box painted to look like a **TREASURE CHEST**

cardboard cut into shape of a **SWORD**

TELESCOPE

painted macaroni for **JEWELS**

paper-covered paper towel roll

upside-down painted egg cartons

SAND — old, brown-speckled sheet over wads of newspaper

Props are the movable items on-stage, from the royal throne to the magic teapot. As you are building these items, remember that the distance between you and your audience works to your advantage. People will not be able to figure out that the gilded jewelry chest is really a cigar box with noodles glued all over it, spray-painted with metallic gold.

Paper plates become fine china, and cardboard tubing with a bit of construction paper turns into a telescope. The way the performers use the objects communicates more to your audience than how they actually appear. Look for throw-away items and transform junk into stage props.

Whether or not you need *costumes* depends on which characters you are portraying. Often street clothes work fine. Look for interesting clothes at

thrift shops, flea markets, and garage sales. You may find outrageous, funny items at low prices. Costumes can be used again and again.

A hint of a costume can go a long way. If you're playing an animal on stage, a few whiskers, cardboard ears, and a tail attached to your jeans suddenly turn you into a mouse, rabbit, or cat. Which one depends on the shape of the ears and the length of the tail. When you create the effect, the audience automatically fills in the rest of the picture.

Sometimes you can use just a hat to indicate a particular character. Hats with feathers, plain ones, baseball caps —each can transform you into a different character. Collect some hats, then write plays to go with them.

Save old sheets and towels. They can be made into capes, long skirts, band-ages, and scarves.

The finishing touch is *makeup*. If you want to appear much older, put a few lines on your forehead with an eyebrow pencil, sprinkle talcum powder on your hair, and add a little red rouge around your eyes. Blue and purple eye shadow create a *primo* black eye.

Get an old tool box to use as a makeup case. Then collect old eye shadow, lipsticks, rouge, and eyebrow pencils. Keep plenty of cold cream and tissues on hand, and be certain to remove all makeup when you are done. That stuff clogs your pores.

To learn how to apply makeup, sit in front of a mirror with a sketch of how you want to look. Try to copy the sketch on your face. Your skill will increase as you practice, and you can be the makeup artist at costume parties as well as for plays.

From Imagination to Backyards

Whenever you're ready, it's show time. You can use any of the ideas in this chapter to put together a collection of plays, pantomimes, skits, and commercials. Performances can be limited to your immediate family and friends or be opened up for next-door neighbors, the people across the hall, or those down the street.

Many a show has been performed in a kitchen or basement with a flashlight for a spotlight. The setting, costumes, and props can be left to the imagination of the audience, or you can go into major production and create a visual world to accompany the words you'll use. Whichever way you choose to go, remember, the play's the thing.

Chapter Eight
Keeping Track of Me

Keeping track of daily life has been going on for a long time. Some professions require it. If you were a ship's captain, you would keep a log of what takes place aboard your ship. Anthropologists write down daily observations, as do scientists and social workers.

Writers frequently keep a diary or journal. It is a special, private place for recording thoughts, feelings, ideas, events, and even the tiniest details of daily life. It's a personal story recorded for your own personal pleasure without your expecting the words to be read by anyone else. You're able to remove all the do's and don'ts and to write just for you.

Occasionally a diary falls into public view. Do you think the everyday life of a person can make interesting reading for others? If you think your life is dull and boring, think again. I'll bet you know at least one hundred real-life stories that would make good reading.

Who Was Samuel Pepys?

Samuel Pepys (say Peeps) lived several hundred years ago in London. On January 1, 1660, at the age of twenty-six, he began keeping a diary of events in his life, and he continued making daily entries for nine years.

To make sure that his writings remained private, Samuel Pepys used a kind of shorthand. Knowing that no one could read his words because of his secret code, he freely included gossip in the details of his daily life, and he even wrote about his secret romances.

His failing eyesight forced Mr. Pepys to stop writing in his diary, and the six volumes sat on his bookshelves until his death in 1703.

Pepys's diaries found a home in a college library and remained untouched until 1818. Finally, a curious man, Lord Grenville, who knew a similar style of shorthand, broke Pepys's code after working on it for just one night. With the code in hand, John Smith, a college student, worked twelve hours a day transcribing Pepys's diaries. Three years and twelve weeks later, Smith finished deciphering the more than one million words that tell the story of an ordinary Englishman.

Pepys's diaries contain much information about the times and customs of the 1600s that were not generally known, in particular, news of the great fire that nearly destroyed London. According to the diary, Pepys first learned of the fire early in the morning hours of September 2, 1666.

"Jane [the housekeeper] called us up, about 3 in the morning, to tell us of a great fire they saw in the City. So I rose and slipped on my night-gowne and went to her window, and thought it to be on the back side of Markelane at the furthest; but being unused to such fires as fallowed, I thought it far enough off, and went to bed again and to sleep."

Many pages of the diary describe the hundreds of buildings—homes, offices, churches—that were consumed by the fire that continued to burn for weeks. He described the fear and how people tried to preserve their belongings. Mr.

Pepys and his wife buried their valuables in a friend's backyard outside London until they could return them safely to their own home. The last mention of the fire was on January 16, 1667 [more than four months after the fire began], where Pepys describes the still-smoldering land.

Pepys's account of the great fire gives details that otherwise would have been lost. Several hundred years after they were written, his diaries continue to inform and delight readers throughout the world.

Dear Diary

A diary can be a notebook, sketchbook, a looseleaf binder full of papers, or a bound book with empty pages. Some diaries have calendar dates already written on each page. Other diaries are absolutely blank.

What you write is up to you. Some people think of their diary as a person. Some even choose to name their quiet friend who absorbs word after word: Dear Oglethorpe (Ogie for short), Dear Yriad (that's diary backwards), or any other name you find suitable will do.

As you begin your diary, there are many choices to make. Will it be private, just for you? Will you keep it under lock and key, or will you bring it out for curious eyes to read? Will you make a concerted effort to write daily or just when the mood strikes you?

There are many ways to begin a diary. Here are a few ideas to get you going or to use on a day when you're not sure what to write.

At This Moment

Describe your surroundings—the chair you're sitting on, the kitchen smells, the textures you see. Then move on to you—how do you feel just now? What are your thoughts? Write them all.

Here I Am

Tell about who you are, through your own eyes and through the eyes of other people. Begin with how you see yourself; then pick a family member and a friend and describe who they see when they look at you.

The People in My Life Today

Make a list of all the people who have entered your life since you last wrote in your diary or journal. If they were characters in a movie, would they be friends or foes, family or strangers? What lines would each one say?

Unfinished Business

Think of what was left unfinished today. Perhaps something was left unsaid to a friend, or a report was left half-done, or a pile of clothes was left on an armchair. Have you any plans for finishing?

Without a Word

Diaries can hold pictures too. Describe your day in pictures. You can use pictographs or, perhaps, a map of today's travels.

What Happened and What If?

All days don't go exactly as we would like them to. On a day that doesn't, write your description of what did happen, followed by a different, imagined series of events.

A Day in Rhyme

Tell your day in a rhyming way. Free verse might be worse.

The Best, the Worst

Of all of the day's experiences, which was the best? the worst?

Pick a Feeling

Make a deck of "feeling" cards by writing a single feeling (happy, sad, bored, angry, frustrated, sleepy, serious, excited, scared, silly, quiet, hurt, confused, peaceful, and so on) on each card (index cards work well). At random, pick a card. Let the feeling written there trigger a memory from the day, then write about it. No memory? Pick another card.

The possibilities for a diary are endless. A diary is a home for whichever words you choose. There is not a single correct way to keep a diary; it is simply your own way. Diaries are like that.

Many Years Away

If you and diarykeeping click, years from now you can sit down with your collection and take a close look. Imagine that it is the year 2005. Has your handwriting changed over the years? Look at the pages for January 7 in each of the years. Is there any pattern in what happened on those days? Check out your birthday for each year. Do you remember the days clearly?

Did your general subject matter stay the same as the years passed? Or did it change? Did you record important news events? Did you write about what happened at school? Did you write about your friends?

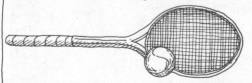

Tennis, Anyone?

When playing an ancient Arabic game, you used your *rahet,* or palm, to hit the ball. And as a player, you were sure to *tanaz*, or leap, around the court. From *tanaz* to tennis — anyone?

Anne and Kitty

When Anne Frank turned thirteen years old, the first birthday gift she opened was a diary from her parents. She named her diary Kitty and said that she would write in it "all kinds of things that lie buried deep in my heart."

Anne described her adventures at school, her best friends, and her family. Then came an abrupt change. Anne and her family had to go into hiding to save their lives. More and more Jews in the city of Amsterdam were being removed, taken away, to forced-labor camps and death camps by the German army. Because they were Jews, the Franks had to hide or risk arrest. The first item Anne packed to take with her was her diary.

For more than two years Anne's life consisted only of her family and four friends and a small hiding place in a secret section of a building. During the confinement she told Kitty what she thought, felt, and did.

The diary came to an end on Tuesday, August 1, 1944, when Nazi soldiers entered the Franks' hiding place and arrested them. Anne died the following spring in a concentration camp. Kitty stayed very much alive in the hands of friends, and Anne's diary has been translated into more than thirty languages and has been read by millions of people.

You can share Anne's secrets by reading her diary. Look for it at your local library.

The History of Me

Is history only what took place hundreds of years ago? Could history have been made last month, last week, or yesterday? Did you make history this morning? History is made with the passing of time. Each passing moment adds to a long story. The word *history* comes from a Greek word having to do with knowledge, learning by inquiry, and being a narrative or story.

What makes history? Do any of the following have a history: baseball, money, television, rock 'n' roll, paper, flowers, buildings, space travel, cars, popcorn, comic books, Australia, sailing, clowns, Mr. Pepys, you?

The answer is yes to all of them. Popcorn, for example, can be traced to early people of the Americas and their 200 varieties of corn, some of which they popped. Comic books have a history dating from 1911 when the very first one was printed. Clowns have a well-traveled history—through the courts of Europe, the streets of Italy, and under the Big Top. So you see, there are as many histories as there are things to talk about.

What about you? The history of your lifetime has many parts, beginning with your birth, continuing all the way to this second. There is a "pre-you" history that led up to your birth. That part of your history links you with the history of other people, relatives and strangers.

Your history is a collection of all the people, places, and events that have been part of a special and unique life—there's only one you.

Remember General Burnsides?

You probably have not heard about his leadership in the Civil War, but his name stuck to the kind of whiskers he liked to wear. They aren't called Generals, and they aren't called Burnsides. Can you guess what they *are* called?

Make a "me wall" on which you can display a collection of all your favorite people, places, and things. Use a bedroom wall or a bulletin board where you can attach photographs of family, friends, and pets. Include magazine cutouts of favorite words or expressions, people you admire, and places you would like to go. Add your own artwork, and before your very eyes, your history will appear.

The Times of My Life

An hour, day, week, or year divides your life into measures of time. Your life gets regulated by these timekeeping devices. You probably eat at certain times of the day, and you know when it's too late to telephone a friend. You count the years to know how old you are. If you "log in" what you do over a short period of time, you will have information to help you estimate what you may do over a long time.

Monday – May 10
6:30 AM – Get up, dress, make bed.
7:00   – Breakfast, brush teeth.
7:45   – Catch bus
8:15   – School
3:15 PM – Home, snack
3:45   – Homework
5:00   – Jean's house
6:00   – Set table
6:15   – Dinner
7:15   – Roller skate
8:00   – T.V.
8:30   – Bed
Tuesday – May 11
6:40 AM – Get up, dress, make bed
7:10   – Breakfast, brush teeth
8:00   – Ride to school with Dad.

Chapter Nine
In Search of . . .

In Search Of . . . that's the name of the finding-out game. Your experience as a "searcher" will come in handy. Maybe you snoop around uncovering neighborhood mysteries, read up on the cause of lightning and thunder, or try to find out the distance from Pluto to Mars, how violins are made, or where Zimbabwe is located. This information may not be found as readily as an answer to the question: What's for dinner? In fact, the best response you may have is: I don't know yet. The *yet* is the key. It means you accept the challenge of the search. This chapter is about ways to find things out.

A Meaning: Look It Up

Imagine you are reading a great book and you find this sentence: People came from far and wide to see the mare, famous for her speed and pulchritude. *Pulchritude?* Reread the sentence a few times. Can you figure out what the word means? What do you do? You could ask someone; he or she might know. Often you are on your own, so search for yourself. Look it up.

To the dictionary you go. Whether it's a large desk version or a small paperback edition, dictionaries give information about words, many words. You can find a code for pronunciation, word history, original meaning or roots, meanings currently associated with that word, and different spellings that are acceptable.

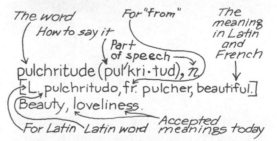

The word
How to say it
For "from"
Part of speech
The meaning in Latin and French
pulchritude (pul′kri·tud), *n.*
[L. pulchritudo, fr. pulcher, beautiful.]
Beauty, loveliness.
For Latin   Latin word   Accepted meanings today

The root section provides clues about how the word came into current use. *Pulchritude* has its roots in Rome as *pulchritudo* in Latin, a word which was derived from the Latin *pulcher*, meaning "beautiful." The English took over

97

from there. This root section tells you *pulchritude* was associated with the idea of beauty from early on. Not so with all words. Sometimes meanings or associations change.

Look up the word *company*. The roots are *com*, meaning "together," and *panis*, the Latin word for "bread." If you combine *com* and *panis*, you break bread when company arrives at your house.

When you look up a word in the dictionary, look at the roots first. Do they give you a hint about the word's meaning? Then look at current meanings. Can you find a connection between the two?

Look up the word *dictionary*. What does the Latin root *dictio* mean? Any guesses as to why the word has its current meaning?

Here's a puzzler for you: Which dictionary can read a book, laugh at jokes, ask questions, and sing? You. You're a walking dictionary. A dictionary holds words, sorts them, collects meanings, knows spellings, and has pronunciations figured out. You do all of these things, and more.

Mice Under My Skin? You've Got to Be Kidding!

Not at all. A mouse of a muscle is better than no muscle at all. The Latin word *musculus*, meaning "little mouse," went to France and became *muscle*. Maybe the French thought the flexing muscle looked like a little mouse moving around under our skin. *Oui?*

Who Parented the Dictionary?

Word collections date back thousands of years to when scholars kept *glosses*, descriptions of word meanings in familiar terms. By the 1500s travelers used special dictionaries to translate words from one language to another.

In 1721 Nathaniel Bailey's dictionary combined word history, use, sentence examples, and illustrations in one book. Samuel Johnson remains famous for his collections of British English, and the first American lexicographer (if you don't know what that word means, look it up), Noah Webster, designed a dictionary to include American pronunciations and spellings, distinctly different from the British ones.

Specialty dictionaries exist for all kinds of categories, such as famous people, food, embroidery stitches, expressions, jokes, rhymes, medical terms, slang, folklore, and that's not all. Look in the reference section in your library to see how many different ones there are.

Lost Words

Lost any words lately? Well, maybe it wasn't you, but someone lost a bundle of them. Read on.

Early one open-tide morn, a backstress woke. Glancing out the eyethurl of her modest cosh, she saw a blue scrow—a good sign for a new day. Still, she had leftover maw-wallop and felt carked. Yesterday's darg produced hardly a chinker! With a ribbled brow, she grabbed her nabcheat and went off to yarken her goods.

The snawk of fresh bread soon filled the streets. A traveling younghede with murfles caught the scent as he entered the town and with a thrip set off to buy some belly-timber.

Did you encounter a few words you don't know? Not surprising. Many are "lost words." Words depend on you and other word-users to keep them in circulation. If not used, words can sit on shelves, getting covered with spider webs until they disappear altogether.

Look in a dictionary for the words *backstress, thrip,* and *murfles.* You probably won't find them. Words can get so lost that dictionaries stop printing them.

Several hundred years ago these Old English words were used regularly in stores, on street corners, and in plays. Today you won't hear them in daily conversation unless *you* throw them in.

If you want to decipher the story and write some more, here's a glossary of lost words to use. Try a couple on your friends. The next time you're playing sports, call for a barlafumble. Tell your pal not to eat too much lubberwort. And remember, no fadoodle.

A Glossary of Lost Words

backstress—female baker
barlafumble—request for time-out
belly-timber—food
breedbate—mischief maker
carked—fretfully anxious
chinkers—money, coins
cosh—hut
darg—day's work
eyethurl—window
fadoodle—nonsense
fellowfeel—sympathize with another
hoful—careful
kew-kaw—upside-down
kissing-comfits—breath fresheners
lip-clap—kissing
lubber-wort—junk food
lulibub—lollipop
malshave—caterpillar
maw-wallop—badly cooked mess of
    food
murfles—freckles
nabcheat—hat, cap
open-tide—early spring
ribble—a wrinkle
scrow—the sky
snawk—to smell
thigging—begging
thrip—finger snap
thrunch—very angry
turngiddy—dizzy
ug—fear, dread
xenodochial—hospitable to strangers
yarken—to prepare
younghede—a youth
zegedine—a drinking cup

backstress

belly-timber

thrunch

lulibub

kew-kaw

People, Places, and Things

If you're seeking information about a person, place, or thing for a school report or just out of natural curiosity, here are some finding-out strategies.

Be a shadow. Do you want to know how to diaper a baby, change a tire, or be mayor of a city? Follow someone who knows how through the task, the way your own shadow follows you. Ask questions as you go along. Afterwards, write up every detail you noticed. If possible, try the task yourself.

This strategy may seem possible with diapering babies and changing tires, but would it be possible in the case of being a mayor? Could be. Many cities have programs designed to teach kids about city government by allowing them to shadow city officials. Call the mayor's office to see if such a program exists or how to get one started.

If you aren't able to hop on a plane that is bound for Istanbul, Nairobi, or Houston, don't give up! You can learn about those places without ever leaving your home town. Local libraries carry books, and often newspapers, from other parts of the United States and the rest of the world.

Try letter writing. Are you interested in some place in the United States? Write to the state capital or to a local city chamber of commerce. Describe what information you want—population, agriculture, business growth, youth programs—and why you want it. Allow a few weeks for the response.

For places outside the United States, write to the country's embassy, which has offices in very large cities. Check with your librarian for the address of the office nearest you.

check the library for magazines from other countries, too.

Try the same technique to gather information about objects too. Do you want to unravel the history of potato chips and how they're made? Check a package of chips to get the company's address. Write a letter, including your questions and the reasons you're asking them. The response may take a few weeks; usually it's worth the wait.

Family Memorabilia

Long ago, among the Kikuyu clan of Kenya, the elders had a special function in the society. Imagine a dispute between two young people. One said, "We're cousins"; the other insisted, "We aren't related; your family came from over the mountain." Who settled it? The elders, since they'd lived the longest and knew the history of the people best of all.

Most important, the Kikuyu elders kept track of marriages, births, and legal matters, all without writing. How did they do it? By remembering and repeating the important events again and again.

Today writing has caused changes among the Kikuyu. The elders remain important, but the records are written.

Who keeps track of important events in your family? Do you know the significant stories: who married whom and where family members were born. You could be the recorder for your family. Begin by compiling questions of what you want to know. Here are some questions to get you started. How are your family members related? How far back can you trace your family history? Where in the world have your family members lived? What kind of work have family members done? What important events have taken place? What are some of the favorite family stories? Try the following methods of gathering information.

Collect Oral Histories

Meet with relatives one at a time, beginning with the elders. Use your questions to assist you in collecting memories of important events and favorite family stories. You can take notes while you listen, writing down just enough key words to help you write it up later. Or you can record the stories for a tape library.

Collecting Histories by Mail

Send written requests for information to out-of-town relatives. Explain what you are collecting and why.

Here's an idea. Say it's your grandmother's seventieth birthday. Make a surprise collection of memorabilia just for her. Ask friends, aunts, uncles, and cousins to contribute writeups of favorite times with Grandma. Place the collection in a decorated box or in a scrapbook. Be sure to add stories of your own.

Chapter Ten
Words to the Future

Does our language have a future? It has certainly come a long way from the early days when pictographs were scrawled on rocks or when each page of a book had to be hand printed. Language is more accessible now than ever before and in various forms— books, newspapers, television, radio, records, movies, and plain old-fashioned conversation. Language continues to adapt and evolve, meeting the ever-changing needs of its human creators.

When you turn back the clock one hundred years and measure the language changes, they have been great. Now the world we live in is faster paced than ever before, and chances are that the changes in the next one hundred years will be even greater than those in the last one hundred.

Which factors will influence change, and what role will you play in all of this? Read on.

The Computers Are Coming

Actually, computers are here. Computers are already in your daily life, making their mark in many different ways. They help pilots fly planes; they play an important role in banking, checking out food at the supermarket, phone calls; and they have a big part in the video arcade.

Chances are you've used a computer in one of its many forms, shapes, and sizes or seen computers in your schools. Today, computer classes are being offered as part of the regular curriculum. Some schools require computer proficiency as a graduation requirement. That could change the course of your educational experience.

There's also the possibility that you are already a computer user, glued to the electronic machine. In case you are not, here's a brief description of computers and how they work.

First, the actual equipment is based on machinery with which you're already familiar—television, tape recorder, and typewriter. Computer equipment includes a monitor (television), recording device (disk, or cassette), and keyboard (typewriter). As the programmer, or computer operator, you type on the keyboard what you want to appear on the monitor screen. That information is memorized on special disks. Another component, the printer, enables the operator to get copies of what has been put into the computer.

The whole operation works because of a tiny chip that is smaller than a fingernail. This computer chip stores thousands of pieces of information and makes a computer do all sorts of extraordinary things.

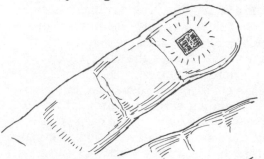

Once you have all the equipment, you still need one more piece of the puzzle to make the computer do what you want: a program. The program could be a Pac-Man game or French lessons. Ready-made programs can be purchased, punched into the computer, then you're on—immediate use. You also have the create-your-own-program option. That option introduces you to the fact that computers have their own language. Once you learn "computerese," the possibilities for using a computer are endless. You can play with it, learn from it, practice problem solving, and use it for creative purposes.

How can what basically appears to be a television and typewriter create such a stir? Appearances can be deceiving because television and computers have one tremendous difference—you *watch* TV; it is a one-way experience that is controlled by the large television networks that create the programs. With computers you *interact,* you take the controls and make things happen.

Following are some activities you can do with a computer.

1. Play arcadelike games that depend on eye/hand coordination and speed.

2. Write stories, plays, poems, letters, and so on. You can store, or keep, your writing on the computer, then go back to make changes and additions. Also, you can get a second copy. That can be a real work saver.

3. Plug into other computers for information. Using a telephone hook-up, computer operators have access to large banks of information on almost any subject. For example, if you had all the necessary equipment, you could make a special call and ask for information about dolphins. Instantly, your monitor would receive the information. It's as if you have a complete library at your fingertips.

4. Make up your own programs. Perhaps you would invent a new intergalactic game or a way to do your algebra homework faster.

**From the Movies
to the Launch Pad**

In an early science-fiction film, *The Lady in the Mirror,* director Fritz Lang used backward counting, or a *countdown,* to start an event: 10-9-8-7-6-5-4-3-2-1 blast off.

Uses for computers far exceed this list, and in the future you can be certain they will extend even farther. Already computers are the main ingredient in our being able to make robots work. In addition, progress is being made on developing computers that can think, and that's a giant change.

It begins to sound as though computers can do almost anything, or, if not, they soon will be able to. Computers do have limitations, and most of those have to do with the fact that they are created by people, and so they can do only what people can do. Also, people make mistakes and can even make mistakes in building and programming computers, so neither people nor computers are perfect.

Do you know something computers *can't* do? Place a computer and a person side by side and make a comparison. Which one can do the following: eat a bowl of buttered popcorn; have fun with you in a pillow fight; send you a postcard from an island in the Caribbean; make you feel safe in a big, old house when you are all alone late at night; help you out if you twist your ankle during a game of field hockey; listen to your problems when you're upset and help you think of some ways to work things out; plan a surprise birthday party for you and invite all your friends; loan you a sleeping bag for a camping trip; call you up in June and say, "Come over to my house right now," and when you get there, bombard you with snowballs that have been in the freezer since January?

Computers are able to do some fantastic things and are wonderful tools for learning and creativity. But will they ever be good substitutes for laughing, talking, thinking, problem-solving friends?

WORD HISTORY

Want a Bar of Chocolatl?

You might not. The Aztec Indians discovered the stuff and used the word *chocolatl,* or "bitter water," to describe the unsweetened flavor of *chocolate.*

The Slang Grows On

"Wow! This is aww-rright, I mean, totally far out. Can you dig where it's at?" If you said that to a shopkeeper in your town one hundred years ago, you'd probably receive quite a stare in return. No one would be able to make sense of your statement; a guess might be that you wanted to purchase a shovel.

Through the years, every generation has made contributions to slang, an ever-changing part of the informal English language. Slang is not an easy word to define, but you usually know it when you hear it.

Slang appears in two basic forms: One is giving old words new meanings, such as "right on" and "far out"; the second is introducing brand-new words into the language, such as "zonked" and "flub-dub." Slang may make its way into the dictionary, but often the words appear and disappear from use so quickly that they are forgotten. Slang words can also change meaning from one group of people to another.

How sharp is your sense of slang? Look at the list of slang and match each word on the left with its corresponding meaning on the right. When you check the answers in the back of the book, you will also find the year of its use.

a.	high mucketymuck	1.	awful
b.	chew the rag	2.	flatter
c.	kick around	3.	entirely
d.	in the soup	4.	satisfactory
e.	shutters up	5.	big shot
f.	butter up	6.	a little money
g.	chicken feed	7.	something extraordinary
h.	copacetic	8.	of little worth
i.	skookum	9.	scold
j.	a sockdolager	10.	in trouble
k.	mouldy	11.	ketchup
l.	short as piecrust	12.	discuss
m.	red lead	13.	employment
n.	all out	14.	keep it secret
o.	bread	15.	extremely short-tempered
p.	dog cheap	16.	excellent

Undoubtedly you use slang in some form or another and will be witness to many slang words as they come and go. Do you think you could intentionally put a new slang word into use and make it catch on? Try it. Gather a few friends and make up a new slang expression; use old words or invent new ones. The fun really begins as you use it with each other and hear it begin to catch on in your family, among friends at school, or wherever you spend your time. Maybe your slang expression will spread like wildfire across the state, even the nation. Slang is definitely here to stay, a part of your present and future, so make your own.

WORD HISTORY

Misickquatash? Delicious!

You may think so too. Living in the area now called New England, the Narragansett Indians ate this mix of corn and beans regularly. The European settlers shortened the name to *succotash.*

The next time you eat zucchini or a pumpkin pie, you're eating a kind of *askutasquash,* according to the Algonquin Indians. Today we call it *squash.*

108

A Question of Gender

There is no doubt that the question of which words to use to describe males and females will be in your future. You have options: Repeat the choices from the past or make changes for the future.

Following are three examples of how words of gender are commonly used today. What do you think of such usage?

1. *Susan and Clark are postmen.* Is Susan really a post*man*? Although she has that job, the title doesn't fit the woman. Recently, the job title was changed. Now Susan and Clark are postal carriers.

Still, the English language has plenty of words that describe jobs and positions by gender. Roles are changing, and the division between men's work and women's work decreases daily. More career options will be open to you in the future. Should our language reflect this change?

2. *Each student must complete his homework.* If that sentence describes an all-male school, then it's accurate. But what if the school is coed? Is the policy at the school different for males and females?

Way back in 1895 Charles Converse, a composer, invented a word that meant both male and female. He took the words *that one* and created "thon," and he used it like this: Every student must complete *thon's* homework. The idea did not catch on. Over the years there have been other suggestions, but they haven't worked either—E, po, xe, and hesh, to name a few.

Here is a list of sentences. Which one would you use to describe students at a coed school where all the students share the same homework rules?

Each student must complete his homework.

Each student must complete her homework.

Each student must complete his or her (her or his) homework.

Each student must complete thon's homework.

All homework must be completed.

3. **Man has lived on planet Earth for millions of years.** True, man has lived on Earth all those years, but he has had company—woman. Many dictionaries define *man* as (1) a male person; and (2) a human being. Is that confusing? Read the following phrase and see what image comes to your mind: Man traveled across the oceans, built homes, and raised food. Do you envision only men? What image comes to your mind with this sentence: Woman traveled across oceans, built homes, and raised food. Are there any men in the second image?

The English language has plenty of words. Can you rewrite the sentences to include males and females in the journey *and* as inhabitants of planet Earth? Do you think it's time to change the dictionary?

When society changes, language changes to keep up with the times. Some people stick to old language habits, complaining, "These changes are too hard. I'm used to the old ways. *Postal carrier, his* and *her*—all that's awkward. I'm not used to it." Other people believe our language has enough words to include females and males equally. Perhaps it is worth being a little awkward to create a more equal world. The words are there; you have only to choose them.

Sticks and Stones

You can't pick up a word and throw it at someone and cause injury, but words can cause hurt nonetheless. You have heard the rhyme: Sticks and stones may break my bones, but words can never hurt me.

Can words hurt? Do you remember a time when someone's words made you feel hurt or sad, ignored or left out, ridiculed or teased, insulted, or angry?

If you have even one memory, join the crowd. You aren't alone. Probably everyone remembers at least one time when words were unfairly spoken to him or her. Words *can* hurt, and it takes time to heal the hurts, just as it does with a broken wrist or a bruised shin.

What causes these unfortunate incidents? Most often, it's people's differences, and differences frequently make people feel uncomfortable at first. Often hurtful words go along with the uncomfortable feelings. The funny thing is that it would be very boring if we all looked, sounded, and thought exactly alike. It is a challenge to accept people's differences and to use words carefully.

Luckily, there's hope. There happens to be a group called "The Word-Wise Kids," dedicated helper-outers in situations when words are tossed about in ways that bruise and break. Who are these models of fair play? Actually, they're normal, everyday kids like you who try to correct misunderstandings and mistakes whenever they can. What do they do? They speak for themselves.

Louise: I began to ask people questions, especially when they seemed different from me. When Elena's family moved into the building, I watched them carry their stuff into the apartment. We couldn't really talk in words because we didn't speak the same language. Actually, it was fun—acting out things and teaching each other phrases. Asking questions helped us get to know each other. I learned from the differences and found out that we have plenty in common.

111

Stan: There was this kid down the block who bullied everyone. Finally, I got fed up and went over to his house and asked him to go to the movies. He was really surprised; in fact, he didn't notice that I was pretty scared. We never made it to the movies; it turns out that he has a great collection of baseball cards.

Fran: I knew that kids at school avoided me because I wore a leg brace. I guess it made them uncomfortable. So one day I brought an extra brace to school and let kids look at it and even try it on. They started asking me about what happened and why I wore it. Things seemed to work out after that.

You Coconut!

Take it easy now, that's a compliment. *Coco* means "smiling face" in both Portuguese and Spanish. So take a coconut and find the three indentations. Those make the face.

Jocelyn: My friend Debbie and I always used to go to the park on Saturdays; sometimes we met other friends there. One day three older kids I had seen at school came over and started calling us racist names. For a while we just stood there, then I said loud and very clearly, "Stop it." Debbie added, "Leave us alone; that's dumb." They mumbled a few more things as they left. Debbie and I talked for a long time about what had happened and how we felt. Then we started brainstorming other things to say, and that made us laugh. We both knew it could happen again and we'd be better prepared the next time.

The Word-Wise Kids are always looking for new members, and it's easy to
join. In fact, you're in already. Read the
following dilemmas and figure out what
you would say.

Share your ideas with family members and friends. What would they do?
Brainstorming—listing ideas without
judging them—can be a great source
for new ideas and strategies. With your
help the future can be safer. Hurting
words can disappear, and we can discover the meaning of three important
French words: *Vive la différence.*

Should This Be Censored?

Prescription medicines carry warnings: KEEP OUT OF THE REACH OF CHILDREN. If taken by accident, some drugs can be extremely dangerous. Adults take extra precaution where your physical safety and health are concerned.

Warnings exist all over—stop signs, handle with care, caution. These warnings are forms of protections.

Should warnings be placed on written materials? DO NOT READ. THESE WORDS MAY HURT YOU.

The issue is censorship. The word *censor* comes from the Latin *censere,* meaning "to assess or judge." Where the written word is concerned, censorship is a judgment about what is being communicated: Is it a bad influence on the reader, is it wrong information, or is it harmful to the welfare of the reader? The result of censorship can be the removal of the censored writing from public view.

Do you think adults should have the right to place warnings on school textbooks, novels, plays, newspapers, or poems the way they do on medicines? Should a book be removed altogether, so you can't see it? Who should make these decisions for you and the rest of your community?

Some adults assume the right of censorship within their own families and even within their communities. Perhaps you have experienced censorship. There are many opinions in the controversy over censorship; here are two.

For Censorship

Adults can best protect the minds of young people and other adults in our community by setting a standard for what's okay to read and what isn't. We decide for everyone. We remove what we don't approve.

For Selection

The Bill of Rights of the United States is based on the belief that we should have freedom of thought and expression. You should have the right to make choices. We don't all have the same standards.

Throughout the United States the battle over censorship continues, especially in schools and libraries. Any written material could be censored, depending on public opinion and laws. That includes what *you* write. Check with your local school board and public libraries to find out where your community stands on censorship. Learn about all sides of the issue.

Chapter Eleven
A Party Full of Words

Words have unlimited uses. You can read, speak, write, and hear with them. They can fill you with emotions at a touching moment in a movie. You can get angry when you hear words of injustice and violence. Words keep you company in the privacy of your own thoughts. Words do all this, and more.

What better chance to find additional ways to play with words than at a party?

An Invitation in Your Own Words

Invitations can be bought at the store or made with your own hands, using your own words. Get a piece of paper and make a list of all the information you want to include in your invitation.

Is this a special occasion—birthday, holiday—or simply a good time to get together? What are the date, time, and location? Do you want to have a theme; come, perhaps, as your favorite word? Should the guests bring something special—favorite poem, sleeping bag, snacks? R.S.V.P.: These letters come from the French phrase "*Répondez s'il vous plaît*," which means "Respond if you please." Do you want to include your telephone number or a message to "tell me at school"? By which date do you want the responses?

Once you have all the information thought out, what form will the invitation take? There's the written variety and the "word-of-mouth" form, which means you invite each friend personally. Written invitations can be in various styles. Here are several ideas to think about.

1. Direct—no fuss, just the facts. "I am having a party on April 24 at my house at 6:00 P.M. I hope you can sleep over. Bring sleeping gear. Please let me know by April 20."

2. Poetic—written in verse, rhyming or not.
"Just couldn't wait
   to celebrate:
Party at eight,
   don't be late!"

3. A task—for your friend to complete. "Unscramble each word to get my message: Rpirsuse Rtayp ofr Raybr!" Or written backwards: "'!yrraB rof ytrap esirpruS"

What do you use for making invitations? Colorful pens, paper, and scissors are essential for creating attractive invitations. Magazines provide pictures and individual letters for a patchwork invitation. You can make each one individually or use a copying machine.

Invitations can be filled with hot air, that is, if you write on a balloon. Or you can mount your invite on thin cardboard and cut it into jigsaw pieces, a puzzle for your friend to assemble. A party proclamation can be written on parchment paper, then mailed in a tube.

An invitation telegram can be made by cutting words out of magazines and pasting them on a sheet of paper. A telegram is sure to capture attention.

Invites can go with your theme; for example, if it's a slumber party and you're rather ambitious, sew tiny pillows, using fabric pens to do the writing.

If you're cohosting the party with a friend, figure out the invitation together. Making the invitations can be as much fun as the party itself.

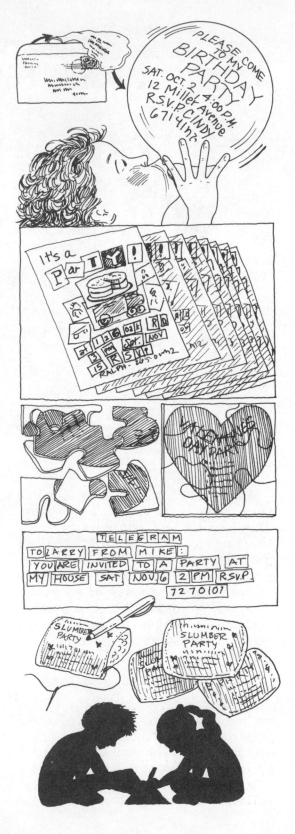

Hidden-Word Hunt

Most of the time we use words without giving them a great deal of thought. But words have built-in fun, and among a group of friends at your party, you can celebrate their many hidden treasures with this hunt.

Get slips of paper and colorful pens. Before your guests arrive, turn your party room into a hunting ground.

1. Hide a surprise somewhere in the room, such as on the top shelf of a tall bookcase.

2. Write a clue about the bookcase location on a slip of paper: "A long librarian finds this spot with ease."

3. Hide the clue under a chair cushion. Then write a clue for that spot: "Some people think I have a cushy job."

4. Hide that clue under the candlestick holder and write another one: "You light up my life!"

5. Keep writing and hiding clues until you have all you want. Don't hide the last clue. Read it aloud to get the hunt started.

6. When someone finds the next clue, read it aloud, then everyone searches for the next clue.

7. The hunt ends when the surprise is found. A batch of cookies is a surprise that everyone can enjoy.

Have a Sandwich, Earl

On August 6, 1762, John Montague, Earl of Sandwich, was too busy gambling to stop for a meal, but he was hungry. His servants brought him a piece of meat tucked between two slices of toasted bread. History records that on August 6, 1762, at 5:00 in the morning, the Earl ate his namesake.

The actual practice of eating food this way dates back nearly 2,000 years, when Rabbi Hillel ate a "sandwich" of flat bread with bitter herbs inside.

I found it!

#3

The Name Game

Are there hidden words in your name? There must be a few. Write your full name: Daphne Carol Dennis, for example. Rearrange the letters to come up with a totally different phrase: Pennie's card had no L. Not all the rearrangements will make sense, but some might. Play this game with your friends and find out what their names mix up to be.

Other kinds of names also can be reassembled to form words. Try to straighten out these names. (The answers are at the back of the book.)

Names of Fruits
1. An A ban
2. Mom ripens
3. No gear
4. Cheap
5. Rant, niece
6. Great nine
7. Later, women

Names of Animals
1. Then leap
2. A boar lake
3. Sneak
4. All Ma

Names of States
1. Taxes
2. Fair oil can
3. We mix once
4. Worn key
5. Wins coins
6. Bear sank
7. Thank at door

Names of U.S. Cities
1. Legal noses
2. Lord Pant
3. All sad
4. Say "cast ink"

Make up more! There are plenty of categories to choose from, such as names of people movers ("real pains" is airplanes) or names of foods.

Word Pyramids

Start with one letter and build a pyramid from the top to the bottom. Add one letter at each step, like this:

a
at
tea
heat
heart
heater
theater

Or, like this one.

a
an
pan
pain
spain
pianos

Build word pyramids with your friends.

Like this??

O
TO
TOW
STOW

No, not like that!

Ever Eat Florence Fries?

Sure, you have. You see, *French fries* originated in Florence, Italy, but were named after the French style of cutting potatoes long and thin.

A Very Moving Game

Two friends volunteer to leave the room to decide on three actions; for instance, talking on the phone, getting dressed, and washing a car. Meanwhile, the rest of the group selects a single word that can describe how people could move—angrily, carefully, quietly, quickly. Let's say the group chooses the word *quickly*.

The two return and say, "Can you talk on the phone this way?" The entire group acts out talking on the phone very quickly.

The pair directs the group to complete each of the three actions. Then comes the guessing—the pair gets three chances to guess the descriptive word. After each round, a new pair leaves the room, and the game starts again.

Handwriting Analysis

Do you dot your letter *i?* Does your handwriting drift upwards? Do your *m*'s have points? All of these characteristics are giveaways to the inner you. Hogwash? Maybe, but maybe not. Graphology, the science of linking handwriting and personality, may guide you to knowing about friends, perfect strangers, and even yourself.

Graphology pops up in all kinds of places. If you apply for a job at a large business, your handwriting may be analyzed to find out if you're dependable or not. As a police officer, you might consult a graphologist to examine kidnap notes or a slip of paper on which is written "This is a stick-up." You can learn the formulas of graphology and use them to delight and amaze friends.

A few words of caution. Graphology can be tricky, especially where young people are concerned. That's because your handwriting is changing. Remember back when you began learning to shape letters at school by tracing in workbooks and copying letter samples? Eventually your perfect little round *o*'s developed a slight tilt and a curlicue on top. Perhaps you developed a rather unique twist in your *s.*

That's no surprise. Your handwriting is in a process of change for years. However your *p*'s and *q*'s end up, they are one of a kind. Absolutely no one else has exactly the same handwriting as you. Graphology may provide clues about you and others while you are changing.

Give unlined sheets of paper to your friends. Ask them to fill half the page by writing about anything at all. Collect the papers and demonstrate your wizardry by using the handwriting clues in the illustration. Of course, there is plenty more to graphology than you have read here. Look for books in the library for more clues, and increase your handwriting wizardry.

Want Some Sarkara Khanda?

If you have a sweet tooth, the answer is probably yes. The words *sugar* and *candy* come from the Sanskrit language in India, *sarkara* and *khanda.*

GUIDE TO GRAPHOLOGY

Look at the following descriptions of handwriting characteristics and what they mean. Do you see your writing in any of the descriptions?

no room all space taken up	Crowded margins: hates to throw things away	*taste*	low t bar: humble, kind
Large	very large writing: extravagant, may be headed for show business	*creative*	high t bar: a dreamer, creative
tiny letters	very small writing: quite intelligent	*optimist*	upslant t bar: optimistic
tight writing	letters clenched together: keeps a secret	*enthused*	t bar more to right: enthusiastic
up up and up	writing slants up: sees the bright side, cheerful, ambitious	*center*	t bar centered: well-balanced
thinker	straight up writing: clear-thinker, self-reliant	*stick*	star shaped t bar: you've got stick-to-it power
large small	large small letters: life of the party	*h l*	no loop: plenty of self confidence
city	not dotted i: may be lazy or careless	*h l*	narrow loop: pretty cautious
artist	circle for a dot: attention to detail	*h l*	high loop: idealistic and ambitious
h u m	flow lines before letters: good sense of humor	*sporty*	long, large loop endings: loves outdoor sports
m n	rounded tops to m or n: may be real cautious	*y g*	no loop: a leader
m n	pointed tops to m or n: energetic, go-getter	*y g*	wide, short loops: may make mountains out of molehills
m n	small line before m or n: temper, temper!	*f*	equal loops top and bottom: good organizer
emply	no cross on t: may be careless	*maybe impractical or imaginative*	many disconnected letters: imaginative and may be impractical

EDIBLE, LEGIBLE EATS

There's an old phrase: You'll eat your words. It's usually said in anger and disagreement and means "You're wrong, and you'll take back what you said." However, in the following activity, you'll eat your words for real.

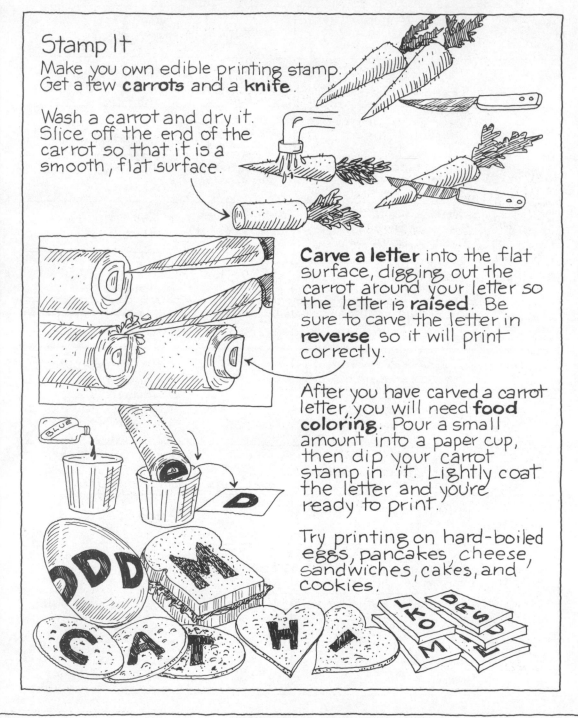

Stamp It

Make you own edible printing stamp. Get a few **carrots** and a **knife**.

Wash a carrot and dry it. Slice off the end of the carrot so that it is a smooth, flat surface.

Carve a letter into the flat surface, digging out the carrot around your letter so the letter is **raised**. Be sure to carve the letter in **reverse** so it will print correctly.

After you have carved a carrot letter, you will need **food coloring**. Pour a small amount into a paper cup, then dip your carrot stamp in it. Lightly coat the letter and you're ready to print.

Try printing on hard-boiled eggs, pancakes, cheese, sandwiches, cakes, and cookies.

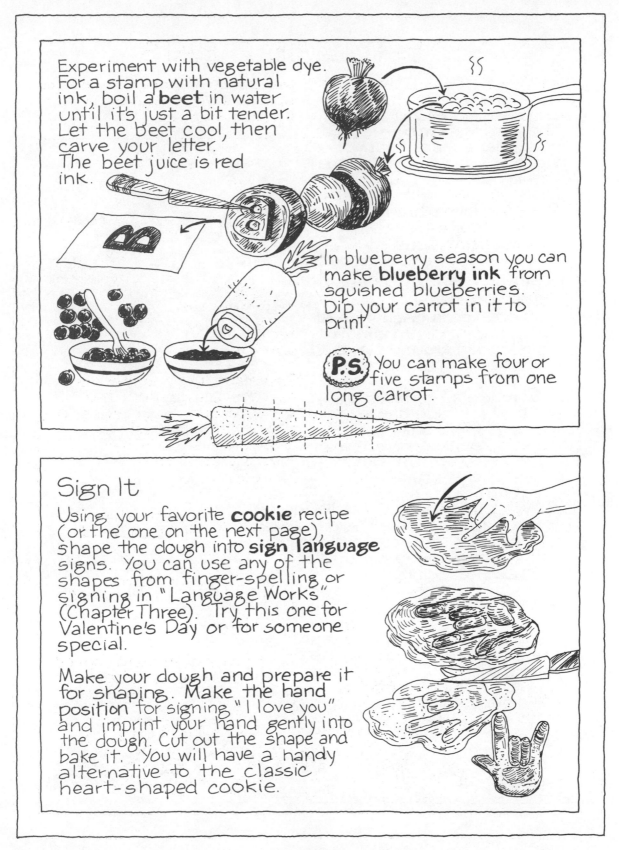

Experiment with vegetable dye. For a stamp with natural ink, boil a **beet** in water until it's just a bit tender. Let the beet cool, then carve your letter. The beet juice is red ink.

In blueberry season you can make **blueberry ink** from squished blueberries. Dip your carrot in it to print.

P.S. You can make four or five stamps from one long carrot.

Sign It

Using your favorite **cookie** recipe (or the one on the next page), shape the dough into **sign language** signs. You can use any of the shapes from finger-spelling or signing in "Language Works" (Chapter Three). Try this one for Valentine's Day or for someone special.

Make your dough and prepare it for shaping. Make the hand position for signing "I love you" and imprint your hand gently into the dough. Cut out the shape and bake it. You will have a handy alternative to the classic heart-shaped cookie.

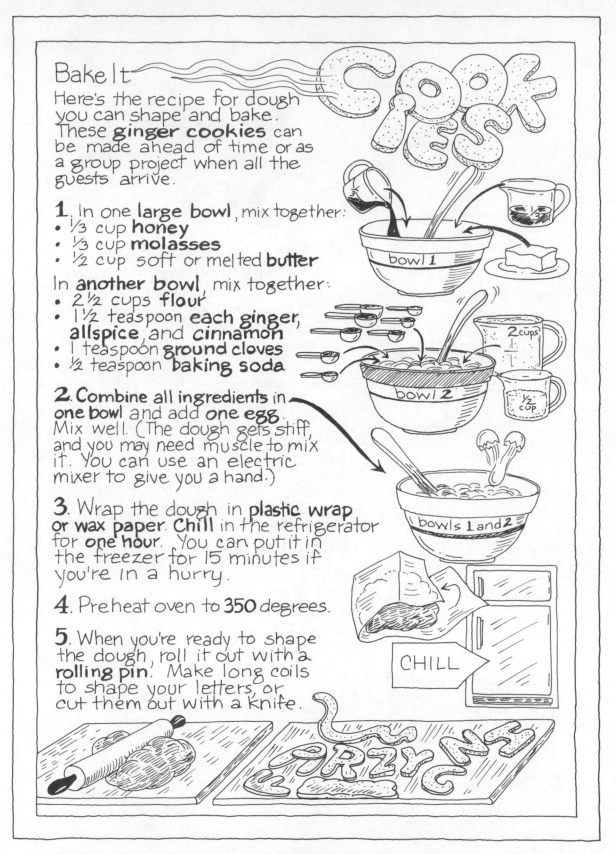

Bake It

Here's the recipe for dough you can shape and bake. These **ginger cookies** can be made ahead of time or as a group project when all the guests arrive.

1. In one **large bowl**, mix together:
- ⅓ cup **honey**
- ⅓ cup **molasses**
- ½ cup soft or melted **butter**

In **another bowl**, mix together:
- 2½ cups **flour**
- 1½ teaspoon **each ginger, allspice**, and **cinnamon**
- 1 teaspoon **ground cloves**
- ½ teaspoon **baking soda**

2. Combine all ingredients in **one bowl** and add **one egg**. Mix well. (The dough gets stiff, and you may need muscle to mix it. You can use an electric mixer to give you a hand.)

3. Wrap the dough in **plastic wrap or wax paper**. **Chill** in the refrigerator for **one hour**. You can put it in the freezer for 15 minutes if you're in a hurry.

4. Preheat oven to **350** degrees.

5. When you're ready to shape the dough, roll it out with a **rolling pin**. Make long coils to shape your letters, or cut them out with a knife.

6. Place your words on a **lightly oiled cookie sheet**. **Bake** for **eight minutes**. **Cool** for **five minutes** on the baking sheet before removing them with a spatula.

Delicious.

PS You may want to cut out the cookies with **cookie cutters** and use your **carrot stamp** to print letters on top.

Bake 8 minutes.

cool 5 minutes.

Two-tone Pancakes

Read your breakfast as you eat it. Here's how.

1. Make 1½ cups of **pancake batter**. Use your favorite recipe. (Recommendation: Go for a simple batter, not one filled with fruit.)

2. Scoop about ¼ cup of the batter into a small bowl. Add 1 tablespoon **milk** to make the batter a little thinner, and 2 tablespoons powdered **cinnamon**. Stir well. The color of the batter will be considerably darker after you add the cinnamon.

3. Prepare to cook. Melt a teaspoon of **butter** in a frying pan. *Remove the pan from the heat.*

4. Get a spoonful of the dark batter and write your initials or a word, dripping the batter from the spoon into the frying pan. Write letters in **reverse**.

mixed batter

1½C

¼CUP

MILK

CINNAMON

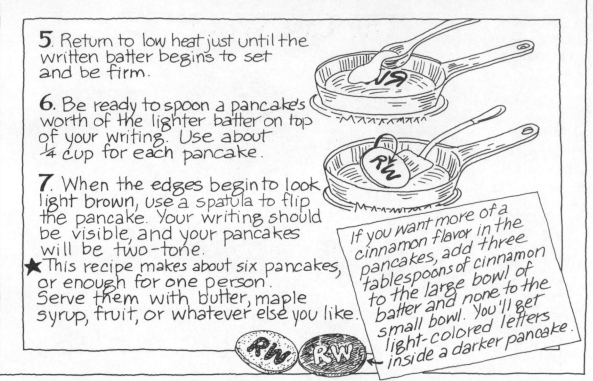

5. Return to low heat just until the written batter begins to set and be firm.

6. Be ready to spoon a pancake's worth of the lighter batter on top of your writing. Use about ¼ cup for each pancake.

7. When the edges begin to look light brown, use a spatula to flip the pancake. Your writing should be visible, and your pancakes will be two-tone.

★ This recipe makes about six pancakes, or enough for one person. Serve them with butter, maple syrup, fruit, or whatever else you like.

If you want more of a cinnamon flavor in the pancakes, add three tablespoons of cinnamon to the large bowl of batter and none to the small bowl. You'll get light-colored letters inside a darker pancake.

WORD HISTORY

Did Graham Go "Crackers"?

Sylvester Graham, 1794 to 1851, a young minister, lectured on the evils of drink and poor diet. Besides recommending vegetarianism, he advocated using unsifted, whole wheat flour. His many followers agreed, and today graham flour is still used for cakes, cookies, and crackers.

A Little Tomato Sauce for My String, Please

A serving of *spaghetti* does resemble a pile of unraveled string, so it's no surprise that its name comes from the Italian *spago* for "cord," or "thread."

If you don't like eating string, try a plate full of worms. *Vermicelli,* that's how you say "little worms" in Italian.

The Last Word

You can't see it, but you've got it. You use it all the time, and there's a chance you take it for granted. Whether it's on the telephone, playing sports, using a computer, or reading a poem, *language* is working for you. Actually, you're an important part of keeping language alive by continually receiving and sending messages.

And you have the delectable morsels of language at your disposal: *words*. They're yours to use, whether you shout them from a mountain top and listen to them echo back or whisper them in a friend's ear. What is more, you're a one-of-a-kind word user; you can be certain no one else will ever use them exactly the way you do. (You're getting more and more important all the time!)

During your lifetime you will use hundreds of millions of words. Do they get tired of you? Do they ever go on strike and refuse to take part in whatever you want to do? Absolutely not. They're always available for singing, rhyming, making up stories, reporting the latest news event, reciting from a stage, talking, and thinking.

Language and words are your friends for life. Keep working with them, and they'll work for you.

Answers

Page 11
Most popular words (in order): the, of, and, a, to, in, is, you, that, it.

Page 13
Top three languages: Chinese, English, Spanish.

Page 19
The pictographs spell: basket.

Page 20
The rebus rhyme says:
I never saw a purple cow
I never hope to see one
But I can tell you anyhow
I'd rather see than be one!

Page 25
The message in code says: I waited at the fountain, but you were late.

Page 27
The Picto-Code message is: I am going to my house. Before I leave, I want to know, can you come over?

Page 28
The Tic-tac-toe Code message is: Happy Birthday.

Page 31
1. This is a great day for a bike ride.
2. There's a fireworks show at the park tonight.
3. Thanks for buying the stamps for me.
4. The dog needs to be walked right away.

Page 44
1. On the bike ride you *hear* the kitten.
2. One bite and you *taste* anchovies.
3. The *sound* of snickering warns you, but it's *touch* that tells you why.
4. One *smell* of beans and you're out of the woods.
5. You catch *sight* of glasses on grandma's head.

Pages 66 and 67
The article about the game doesn't say who won, nor does it give the winning score. The article about the volcano doesn't tell where the volcano is nor when it erupted. The article about the young scientists doesn't include information about what they made that earned the award for them.

Page 107
a. high mucketymuck (1905): 5. big shot
b. chew the rag (1885): 9. scold
c. kick around (1947): 12. discuss
d. in the soup (1889): 10. in trouble
e. shutters up (1850s): 14. keep it secret
f. butter up (1930s): 2. flatter
g. chicken feed (1836): 6. a little money
h. copacetic (1933): 4. satisfactory
i. skookum (1913): 16. excellent
j. a sockdolager (1869): 7. something extraordinary
k. mouldy (1890s): 1. awful
l. short as piecrust (1849: 15. extremely short-tempered.
m. red lead (1928): 11. ketchup
n. all out (1300): 3. entirely
o. bread (1785): 13. employment
p. dog cheap (1616): 8. of little worth

Page 118
Names of fruits: 1. banana, 2. persimmon, 3. orange, 4. peach, 5. nectarine, 6. tangerine, 7. watermelon.

Names of animals: 1. elephant, 2. koala bear, 3. snake, 4. llama.

Names of states: 1. Texas, 2. California, 3. New Mexico, 4. New York, 5. Wisconsin, 6. Nebraska, 7. North Dakota.

Names of U.S. cities: 1. Los Angeles, 2. Portland, 3. Dallas, 4. Kansas City.